THE
C-SPAN
ARCHIVES

*An Interdisciplinary Resource for
Discovery, Learning, and Engagement*

THE C-SPAN ARCHIVES

An Interdisciplinary Resource for Discovery, Learning, and Engagement

edited by
ROBERT X. BROWNING

PURDUE UNIVERSITY PRESS, WEST LAFAYETTE, INDIANA

Copyright 2014 by Robert X. Browning. All rights reserved.
Printed in the United States of America.

Library of Congress Cataloging-in-Publication Data

The C-SPAN archives : an interdisciplinary resource for discovery, learning, and engagement / edited by Robert X. Browning.
   pages cm
  Includes bibliographical references and index.
   ISBN 978-1-55753-695-2 (paperback) — ISBN 978-1-61249-353-4 (epdf) — ISBN 978-1-61249-354-1 (epub) 1. C-SPAN (Television network)—Archives. 2. Public affairs television programs—United States—Archives. 3. United States—Politics and government—1977-1981. 4. United States—Politics and government—1981-1989. 5. United States—Politics and government—1989-1993. 6. United States—Politics and government—2001-2009. 7. United States—Politics and government—2009- I. Browning, Robert X, 1950- editor.
  PN1992.92.C2C74 2014
  384.55'5—dc23
                     2014021342

To David A. Caputo.
Colleague. Mentor. Friend.

CONTENTS

FOREWORD *xi*
PREFACE *xiii*

PART I *Overview of C-SPAN and the C-SPAN Archives*

CHAPTER 1
    Introduction to C-SPAN, Its Mission, and Its Academic
        Commitment *3*
Susan Swain

CHAPTER 2
    Introduction to the C-SPAN Video Library *7*
Robert X. Browning

CHAPTER 3
    C-SPAN's Origins and Place in History: Personal Commentary *15*
Brian Lamb

PART II *Research Case Studies Using Rhetorical and Historical Lenses*

CHAPTER 4
    Preserving Black Political Agency in the Age of Obama: Utilizing the
        C-SPAN Video Archives in Rhetorical Scholarship *29*
Theon E. Hill

CHAPTER 5
    Going Beyond the Headlines: The C-SPAN Archives, *Grassroots '84,* and
        New Directions in American Political History *45*
Kathryn Cramer Brownell

CHAPTER 6
Deference in the District: An Analysis of Congressional Town Hall Meetings From the C-SPAN Video Library   *59*
Colene J. Lind

PART III   *Research Case Studies Using Social Scientific Lenses*

CHAPTER 7
Using the C-SPAN Archives to Enhance the Production and Dissemination of News   *81*
Stephanie E. Bor

CHAPTER 8
Measuring Emotion in Public Figures Using the C-SPAN Archives   *93*
Christopher Kowal

CHAPTER 9
A Social Practice Capital to Enhance the C-SPAN Archives to Support Public Affairs Programming   *109*
Sorin Adam Matei

PART IV   *Teaching Case Studies*

CHAPTER 10
Using the C-SPAN Archives to Teach Mass Communication Theory   *123*
Glenn G. Sparks

CHAPTER 11
Teaching American Government Concepts Using C-SPAN   *133*
Robert X. Browning

CHAPTER 12
Interactive Learning In and Out of the Classroom   *141*
Robert X. Browning

CHAPTER 13
Designing and Teaching Multidisciplinary Project-Based Teams Using the C-SPAN Archives   *145*
William Oakes, Carla Zoltowksi, Patrice M. Buzzanell

PART V   *Future Possibilities*

CHAPTER 14
   Partisanship Without Alternatives: Keynote Reflections on C-SPAN and My Mother   *155*
   Roderick P. Hart

CHAPTER 15
   Reflections on the Potential and Challenges of the C-SPAN Archives for Discovery, Learning, and Engagement   *169*
   Patrice M. Buzzanell

REFERENCES   *179*
CONTRIBUTORS   *195*
INDEX   *201*

FOREWORD

I am pleased to have been given the opportunity to write the Foreword for this important volume exploring the rich resources of the C-SPAN Archives. As a former president of the National Communication Association (NCA), I am particularly pleased that the NCA provided the venue for the conference that was the impetus for this book. I believe both the conference and the book offer a compelling window into the valuable archive held by C-SPAN. And, as you read this volume, I think you will see how rich the C-SPAN Archives is, and how much promise it holds for future research and pedagogy.

This book clarifies how what's been communicated via C-SPAN shapes further communication among people. It is extremely useful to read a volume that spans research endeavors and pedagogy as well as political issues, and, in addition, projects into people's everyday lives. While any event, such as a presidential speech, for instance, has implications for all these arenas, this book is one of the few in my experience that focus on all these dimensions, explicitly showing how research, teaching, and practical application naturally intertwine. Further, the well-defined multidisciplinary focus of this book is an invaluable contribution. Universities currently focus on the importance of bringing a variety of disciplines together to think through seemingly intractable problems. This volume illustrates how different disciplines can illuminate the texts provided by the C-SPAN Archives. Engaged scholarship and partnerships between community and university personnel are often-invoked buzzwords in education today. But this volume makes these phrases come alive and embodies them with purpose, showing how the communication of political ideas permeates our experience and offers possibilities for edification and change.

This book features chapter topics as widely disparate as a rhetorical analysis of black political agency in the age of Barack Obama's presidency, and an essay illustrating ways to use the C-SPAN Archives to teach mass communication theory. Through this diversity, the book illustrates the richness and depth of the C-SPAN Archives for scholars, teachers, and citizens. To have access to the raw data of nearly 30 years of the political history of the United States allows for research and teaching uses limited only by our imaginations. The variety of scholarship demonstrated within this volume is exciting and thought provoking. It provides a window into the C-SPAN Archives and a window into our political and mediated lives. It allows us to focus on the big picture and to drill down to specifics. It provides us with a beginning, and a promise that there is much more to follow. I, for one, am thrilled with this book, and the prospect of more to follow. I invite you to enjoy the range and depth of what is contained in this volume. It will be an exciting read, inspiring you to think about politics, communication, and life in our contemporary world in many different ways. I cannot think of a better use of our time and energy.

Lynn H. Turner, Past-President, National Communication Association

PREFACE

The impetus for this edited collection actually began many years ago. As a Purdue University alum, Brian Lamb encouraged the university to set up an archive for the C-SPAN programming at his alma mater; Robert Browning set up the technological systems to digitize these materials into the C-SPAN Video Library (also known as the C-SPAN Archives) to provide free access worldwide; and Howard Sypher and Irwin (Bud) Weiser, as head of the Department of Communication and dean of the College of Liberal Arts, respectively, envisioned and started to talk about naming a school in honor of Brian Lamb. To celebrate these events, several faculty—Patrice Buzzanell, Glenn Sparks, Robert Browning, and Steve Wilson, then interim head of the Department of Communication—met to talk about ways to highlight the possibilities that came with the naming of a Lamb school at Purdue.

These conversations converged into a vision for creating awareness and encouraging use of the C-SPAN Archives. This vision was designed to further the C-SPAN Archives' use not only for engaged scholarship and teaching in communication, political science, and other disciplines but also for tracing U.S. governmental discourses, policies, and major political-economic and social events by anyone interested in these facets of American life. Put differently, the vision involved the creation of greater connections within communication and across disciplines by focusing on the C-SPAN Archives, not solely as historical and political materials, but also as a window into the everyday issues and opportunities that shape (and are shaped by) contemporary life for citizens of the United States and the globe.

Some of the challenges in achieving this vision included finding venues in which researchers, teachers, media specialists, archivists and librarians, and nonacademic parties could interact meaningfully in ways that would be precise enough to be productive for scholarly audiences and conversational enough to appeal to broader groups. In addition, there needed to be a sustainable system for achieving multiple goals. The approach to these issues involved a two-part strategy. The first part necessitated establishing an annual conference and distinguished lecture that would promote use of the C-SPAN Archives and provide the bases for different kinds of outputs, such as this book. The second part was finding a publisher that would enable free online access to the book and online materials after a year and that would sign on for a series of edited collections that could begin with this sourcebook and evolve into different and more complex outputs as the C-SPAN Archives became more prominent in discovery, learning, and engagement, as well as popular use.

These aspects came together in the fall of 2013 when Patrice, Robert, and Glenn co-organized a daylong National Communication Association (NCA) Preconference in Washington, DC, at the C-SPAN headquarters and Purdue University Press agreed to publish the proceedings. The preconference and this resulting book focused on and continued to explore the unique research possibilities, innovative teaching techniques, and engagement for policy and other outcomes afforded by the Archives' use.

WHY HAVE AN EDITED COLLECTION FOCUSED ON THE C-SPAN ARCHIVES?

To meet multiple objectives and audiences, this book demonstrates how individuals and groups can use the C-SPAN Archives as a rich, primary source and where there might be opportunities for multidisciplinary collaboration across contexts and different methodologies.

C-SPAN provides daily coverage of speeches, debates, forums, and events in which public officials—the leaders of U.S. democracy and in other contexts—provide a record. This coverage reaches more than 90 million U.S. households through three 24-hour television networks—C-SPAN, C-SPAN2, and C-SPAN3—providing daily records of the U.S. House of Representatives and Senate as well as congressional hearings, presidential speeches, White House briefings, news conferences, policy seminars, and other events.

Since 1987, the C-SPAN Video Library has preserved this audio and video record without editing or commentary, indexed and readily accessible in digital form through the C-SPAN Video Library (http://www.c-span.org/blog/?3440). Over 200,000 hours of C-SPAN programming dating back to 1980 are available. The Video Library allows for searching, clipping, sharing, and downloading. The process for doing this research is outlined in this book.

Yet the C-SPAN Archives has not been fully utilized. Even this edited collection contains only a few possibilities for scholarship and everyday research. It is the hope of those who created the original NCA preconference that future work showcase possibilities for communication and interdisciplinary scholarship that integrates discovery, learning, and engagement, that utilizes multiple methodologies, and that touches upon diverse communication, political science, and other contexts ranging from K–12 initiatives that can encourage civic engagement to immigration debates, environmental and health challenges, human rights, institutional policies, and corporate social responsibility, amongst others of a local through global nature.

WHY NOW?

There are several reasons that the C-SPAN Archives and its use are of particular importance at this time. Primary is that understanding how use of the C-SPAN Archives is and can be further situated within contemporary higher education enables scholars and nonacademics to leverage different aspects to benefit students, singular disciplines and multidisciplinary projects, funded programs, and so on. Because higher education and global informational needs are changing, further reasons that the C-SPAN Video Library is significant now include (a) access to unedited digital content and (b) utilization for engaged scholarship and academic-community partnerships.

ACCESS TO UNEDITED DIGITAL CONTENT

Although it has been mentioned earlier and the authors of the chapters in this book discuss the point, it still bears repeating that the C-SPAN Video Library does not contain reconstituted and previously framed information. As well as historically significant testimony and speeches, the C-SPAN Archives also contains fairly routine governmental events, hearings, question-answer sessions, asides, and political interactions in their original form. It is in the mundane actions of speakers at hearings, officials presenting talks, and so on that individuals can see their government in action. They can hear and see policy being made and the decision making that evolves and coalesces into laws and statements of rights. In short, C-SPAN exposes the informational infrastructure of political, economic, and social decisions that impact people every day.

In today's world of news entertainment and high viewership requirements, the fact that these materials are unaltered but certainly embedded in political and other contextual understandings—recessions and years of prosperity, welfare policies, First Lady involvement in national campaigns, and White House initiatives—offers unique views into American political life. The temporal and spatial ordering unfolds as it did during the actual occurrences.

The primary archival data can be captured into secondary data infrastructures based on individuals' purposes as singular and/or multiple databases with video footage and captioning. These materials offer the raw data upon which arguments have been based and that can be scrutinized by scholars and nonacademics. The C-SPAN Archives content also is part of the popular cultural landscape since it is used in advertisements, movies, YouTube videos, and other materials.

UTILIZATION FOR ENGAGED SCHOLARSHIP AND ACADEMIC-COMMUNITY PARTNERSHIPS

Over the last decade and more, there has been increasing urgency to develop partnerships between researchers and different groups that need professional expertise to help solve problems and contribute in meaningful ways to issues affecting local and global communities. Using theories and empirical findings as resources, engaged scholars have helped shape processes, policies, and practices of everyday life and our future.

Engaged scholarship is not simply traditional research applied to various settings. Rather, engaged scholarship alters the learning-discovery processes and operates as partnerships. Engaged scholarship often does not promote the researcher-as-sole-expert model, nor does it necessarily highlight a particular discipline. Engaged scholarship often is multidisciplinary, team oriented, community embedded and relationship oriented, and interested in discovery from the ground up. It may also be funded with observable deliverables and sustainability issues embedded in its design.

The relationship of engaged scholarship and partnerships to the C-SPAN Video Library is that this archive offers the means by which scholars and community members can pursue increased civic involvement and knowledge in a form that is immediate and easily ascertainable. Partnering with and developing expertise in different stakeholders helps local communities but also the nation and world as a whole—reaching out to different publics, noting shifting public discourses, learning how governmental framing might preclude other ways of seeing issues and their positionings vis-à-vis national and global conflicts, and imagining other possibilities for the Archives' use.

Engaged scholarship and academic-community partnerships are initiatives aligned with key directions toward which universities and funding agencies have been headed for years. Many stakeholders want research that moves out of the labs and into everyday practice. Many stakeholders also want engaged and relevant teaching. The C-SPAN Archives provides the materials for classroom and training use aligned with engaged teaching and deep learning. In short, the C-SPAN Archives offers a site in which the unique intersections of discovery, learning, and engagement involving members of the academy and nonacademics can converge.

HOW IS THE C-SPAN ARCHIVES INITIATIVE MOVING FORWARD?

In this section, an outline for upcoming conferences and edited collections is provided as well as the audience for these materials. A note of appreciation to those who made all of this possible closes this Preface.

Upcoming Conferences and Edited Collections

Now that it is almost a year since the beginnings of this project, it is time to look back and assess this work, the original goals and vision, and the ways in which the C-SPAN Archives initiative is moving forward. As this book is being completed, microgrants are being awarded to individuals in communication, political science, library science, history, journalism, and other fields for conducting research using the C-SPAN Archives. These grants have resulted from the generous support of the C-SPAN Education Foundation and the commitment of various schools and offices at Purdue University to match C-SPAN funds. Specifically, Purdue University President Mitch Daniels agreed to provide the requested amount from the president's contingency fund as a match to the funding the C-SPAN Foundation has provided.

In accepting the peer-reviewed and competitively selected grants for C-SPAN Archives research projects, awardees have indicated their interest in attending a conference at Purdue University to present their findings. Like the content and format of the inaugural C-SPAN Archives conference, this second conference would offer fresh visions for future research that enriches and broadens the Archives' use. These presentations also would be recorded and organized into chapters for a second volume of the C-SPAN Archives series. A third conference is being planned for the summer of 2015.

Audience for This Book

It is the hope of the contributing authors that students, teachers, librarians and archivists, and researchers will find this book intellectually stimulating and useful. Beyond sharing classroom and research projects, contributors want to stretch boundaries. In particular, the contributors expect that this book will encourage conversations within and across academic disciplinary boundaries. The Archives can facilitate community mobilization, public health policymaking, and arguments for funded research and can inform politically and socially conscious individuals.

The materials within this book only hint at current work and future possibilities. The originators of this conference and book series are still grappling with finding optimal ways of promoting interest in and use of the C-SPAN Archives. What contributors to this volume already have done with the Archives is both inspiring and humbling; what the projects for the second C-SPAN Archives conference plan to deliver—even more so.

Sincere Appreciation

Of the many people who deserve sincere appreciation for their efforts on behalf of the C-SPAN Archives conference and this edited collection, a few are listed below.

First and foremost is Brian Lamb, who encouraged the C-SPAN Archives and lent his name to the School of Communication at Purdue University. Susan Swain and C-SPAN provided access to the headquarters, to staff, and to limitless coffee for the 2013 NCA Preconference. At C-SPAN, the key contact was Donald Hirsch, whose patience, good humor, and assistance in accomplishing a smoothly running preconference were incredible. Among other C-SPAN contributions to the conference and this book, Kristina Buddenhagen and Kenneth (KJ) Carrick spent many hours blocking out the room, setting up equipment, and recording the 2013 conference. Slade Horacek, C-SPAN administration specialist, kept an eye on things throughout the preconference day in case anything was needed or wanted and provided one of the highlights of the day—namely, a personal tour of the C-SPAN facilities with plenty of photo ops. Joel Bacon and Christina Whirl provided access to the conference facilities and to prized giveaways such as C-SPAN mugs for all participants. In this endeavor, C-SPAN's support in terms of time, energy, personnel, and funds was—and continues to be—considerable.

Second, the National Communication Association not only enabled the conference organizers to publicize this event and access its online registration system, but also provided an additional panel, the DC Connections, to generate onsite NCA conference interest in the C-SPAN Archives. Thanks to Michelle Randall, Trevor Parry-Giles, Teresa Bergman (NCA preconference planner for 2013), and Ted Sheckels (DC Connections planner).

Third, thanks go to the Brian Lamb School of Communication for support and involvement. Marifran Mattson, then interim head of the school, okayed the honorarium and plaque for the keynote speaker, Rod Hart, and Donna Wireman helped order food and materials. Ziyu Long set up the Dropboxes. Charles Watkinson, then director of the Purdue University Press and head of Scholarly Publishing Services at the Purdue University Libraries enthusiastically welcomed the initial idea for the book and shepherded the project through the early phases. Charles and his superb staff deserve utmost appreciation. In particular, Kelley Kimm was a skillful copy editor and facilitator who ensured that this book stayed on deadline for publication. Katherine Purple and Judy Rantz ensured that the administrative details were all met and that the production and promotion occurred on schedule. Without this superb team, this book would never have achieved its ambitious timetable. Without the C-SPAN Archives staff, conference participants, presenters, colleagues, and book authors, none of this would have happened—many thanks!

FINAL NOTES

From Robert

On the writing side, Patrice Buzzanell was an unending source of ideas, encouragement, editing, and inspiration. Every book needs a Patrice behind it.

And on a final note, David A. Caputo, former dean of the Purdue University School of Liberal Arts, deserves special recognition. When I first took the idea of the Archives to him in 1987, he was enthusiastic and supportive, and he provided the resources to get us started. Without his administrative support and professional encouragement, this endeavor would not have been possible and the research, teaching, and engagement possibilities set forth here would not exist. Thank you, David. This book is dedicated to you.

From Patrice

It has been such a pleasure to work with Robert on the organizational details for the NCA Preconference and for this edited collection. As his associate editor, I have greatly appreciated his incredible political knowledge and dedication to the C-SPAN Archives. I also enjoyed contributing to the chapters on EPICS and the concluding chapter—*thank you Robert!* I have learned so much from him about the C-SPAN operation overall and the political-social impetus that brought the C-SPAN Archives to the national (and international) treasure that it is today.

Robert X. Browning, Editor
Patrice M. Buzzanell, Associate Editor
May 2014

PART I

OVERVIEW OF C-SPAN AND THE C-SPAN ARCHIVES

CHAPTER 1

INTRODUCTION TO C-SPAN, ITS MISSION, AND ITS ACADEMIC COMMITMENT

Susan Swain, President and Co-CEO, C-SPAN

In November 2013, faculty from the Brian Lamb School of Communication at Purdue University organized a session in Washington, DC, attached to the annual gathering of the National Communication Association. Their goal was to demonstrate to members of the academy the richness of the C-SPAN Video Library (http://www.c-span.org) for both academic research and teaching. This book is a result of that daylong session.

This project is a long time coming. Academic use of the C-SPAN video collection has always been a goal of the network and, in particular, of the collection's founding director, Dr. Robert Browning. The archival systems he and his team created for the C-SPAN Video Library were initially developed with an eye toward academic research, and while the C-SPAN viewing audience has embraced the use of the online Video Library, academic use has much greater potential. We hope this project creates a foundation for it to grow.

A bit of background about C-SPAN and its Video Library may be useful. C-SPAN first went on satellite in March 1979, created as a public service by the nation's cable television companies and organized as a not-for-profit company to distribute noncommercial public affairs programming to our affiliates. Although our mission is to televise the workings of the federal government, it's important to note that C-SPAN is a private company that neither seeks nor receives public funding. We began by televising the floor debates of the U.S. House of Representatives, live and without commentary, allowing the American public to see for themselves the workings of Congress. As amazing as it seems in today's world where video is ubiquitous, the 1977 debate over allowing television access to the halls of Congress was hard fought; both its proponents and detractors understood that the idea was revolutionary. Soon after its launch, C-SPAN began to add additional content, such as live interview/call-in programs and coverage of congressional hearings. By 1986, the U.S. Senate found itself relegated to the sidelines of news coverage and decided to allow television cameras to cover its debates, as well. C-SPAN2 was launched in June of that year to carry the Senate live.

The year 1986 was notable for another reason: a discussion took place between the College of Liberal Arts faculty at Purdue University and C-SPAN founder and Purdue alumnus, Brian Lamb, which led to the creation of the C-SPAN Video Archives. Mr. Lamb lamented that C-SPAN was regularly forced to erase historic political video because no system existed for capturing and archiving it. Dr. Browning, then an assistant professor of political science, raised his hand and volunteered to develop such a system. With the backing of his dean, Dr. David Caputo, Dr. Browning launched the C-SPAN Archives in September 1987 and has accomplished the herculean task of capturing every event televised by C-SPAN in the ensuing 27 years.

In 1998, an agreement between Purdue and C-SPAN brought the Archives under C-SPAN's control and the organization moved off campus to its current home in the Purdue Research Park in West Lafayette, Indiana. The long relationship between Purdue University and C-SPAN remains vibrant, highlighted by the naming of the Brian Lamb School of Communication in 2011.

The C-SPAN Archives currently contains more than 200,000 hours of video content. In this vast collection are the public events of five presidents, complete video records of the floor debates of each Congress from the 101st onward, candidate events from seven presidential campaigns, and hundreds of hours of public and official reaction to major historical events. A quick tap of our collective memories illustrates the richness of the materials: the Iran-Contra Investigation; the Robert Bork and Clarence Thomas nominations; the Persian Gulf War; NAFTA; the end of the Cold War; the Oklahoma City bombing; the Clinton impeachment trial; the Columbine and Sandy Hook school shootings; the 2000 recount; 9/11; Enron; the Columbia explosion; the Iraq and Afghanistan Wars; Hurricane Katrina; the Abramoff lobbying scandal; the 2008 financial crisis; the Arab Spring; the same-sex marriage debate; the passage of the Affordable Care Act; and federal budget standoffs too numerous to list. In short, at one's fingertips is a cache of nearly 30 years of U.S. political history in original source format—long-form coverage of events without commentary. The threads of potential research available to any interested political scientist seem almost overwhelming.

And, as time passes, historians will also find that they can come to the Video Library to find oral histories, the reminiscences of political leaders, and firsthand accounts of the events of the past 30 years.

Researchers and teachers in the communication fields will find much to harvest as well. Because the policy debate is fueled by political rhetoric, the C-SPAN Archives is a treasure trove for the study of social and political argument. Students of advertising and public relations will find public campaigns on major policy issues and several decades' worth of political advertisements. Health communication researchers can examine the public debate over issues as impactful as stem cell research and as current as toy safety during the holidays. Not surprisingly, there are literally hundreds of hours of video available on key health policy topics such as HIV/AIDS research, research funding for cancer, and abortion.

Also part of the Archives' collection is the content produced by C-SPAN's *BookTV* unit, which offers 48 hours of programming about nonfiction books each week. Nearly every significant nonfiction author of the past 15 years has been captured by its cameras. Likewise, the primary source video produced by C-SPAN's most recent programming venture, *American History TV*, has been captured and organized by the C-SPAN Archives.

Amassing this collection since 1987 has been both a technological challenge and a labor of love for Dr. Browning and his staff. As video technology changed from half-inch tapes collected by VCRs to digital files swept in by servers, the Archives had to change, too, and then update all the materials that came before. The two most profound decisions in the history of the Archives were its initial founding in 1987 and the 2005 decision by C-SPAN's board of directors to fund the complete digitization of the network's video collection and make it fully available to the public.

This latter decision was a significant contribution to the public good on the part of the cable television industry, which created and funds C-SPAN operations. Today, in ways that were not possible for much of the Archives' prior history, one can easily access and use the C-SPAN Video Library from a desktop computer or mobile device. Closed captioning–based transcripts make keyword searches possible; online tools make clipping and sharing video as simple as a few clicks on the keyboard.

Using the Archives' digitized collection and the online Video Library's search tools, the contributors to this book hope to demonstrate the application of C-SPAN video to specific research studies and to coursework. All of us involved in this project hope to further spread the word about the rich content available in the Video Library and to stimulate interest in C-SPAN–based teaching and research.

Thank you for your interest in this first-of-its kind effort, to the National Communication Association for its support, and to the Lamb School faculty organizers of this project, particularly Dr. Patrice Buzzanell, Dr. Glenn Sparks, Dr. Howard Sypher, and Dr. Robert Browning, the editor of this volume.

As the old saying goes, may what you read on these pages allow a thousand flowers to bloom.

CHAPTER 2

INTRODUCTION TO THE C-SPAN VIDEO LIBRARY

Robert X. Browning, Purdue University and C-SPAN Archives

There was an early recognition that C-SPAN programming is important content to be preserved. As Susan Swain indicates in Chapter 1, "Introduction to C-SPAN, Its Mission, and Its Academic Commitment," the topic came up early in a discussion with Purdue University faculty in 1986. By that time, C-SPAN was seven years old, was programming two networks, and was aware that what it was creating through its daily, unedited coverage of Washington, DC, public affairs events was a valuable, historical recognition of the nation's history.

C-SPAN programming includes the entirety of House and Senate legislative sessions, congressional hearings, news conferences, presidential speeches and other appearances, party conventions and campaign events, many public policy forums, and daily call-ins with elected officials, policy leaders, and journalists. Because of the unedited nature of C-SPAN's programming, as well as its balanced selection of events and production values that do not detract from or try to influence these events, the coverage that C-SPAN creates serves as much more than the first draft of history. It is the video record of the nation's policymaking and discussion of that policy.

The archive that we envisioned was to be an indexed video collection of primary event coverage. Initially, it was a collection of videotapes with a computerized index to those videos. That initial vision and the basic architecture allowed the collection to develop into the C-SPAN Video Library (http://www.c-span.org), a digitally indexed and accessible collection of more than 200,000 first-run C-SPAN hours aired since 1987.

The technology that was used in the early days was not complex. Twelve VHS recorders captured each network 24 hours a day, 7 days per week on 2-hour videotapes. Today, the technology is much more complex, but it uses the same principles that guided the earliest architecture. Digital encoders create 1-hour files that are stored on servers, then processed into different viewing formats, moved onto the storage RAIDs (redundant arrays of independent drives), copied to Amazon Web Services in the cloud for redundancy, and backed up in the original high format on the digital tapes. An additional recording stream creates 5-minute files so that the video can be almost instantaneously available. Many archives have a lag time before materials are available; we keep that lag down to about 10 minutes after an event begins.

While we moved from analog tapes to digital files in 2002, one thing that has remained constant in both the analog and digital eras has been the use of a core database to manage all the information about the video recording. From the first days, we began organizing the information into fields and entering these data first into a single computer and later into a networked database that allowed different people to enter data at the same time. This decision created a retrieval system that could be used to quickly find and duplicate the videotapes and answer questions about what videos we had in response to telephone inquiries.

It is easy to see how this indexed system became the basis for C-SPAN Video Library in 2010—a move that won the C-SPAN Archives a George Foster Peabody Award for excellence in digital journalism. The relationship between the video and the database records was a critical organizational decision that allowed the Archives to retrieve and digitize the 120,000 hours of analog content—once C-SPAN's board of directors made the decision to build the Video Library of all available C-SPAN content. When that content was digitized and available online, 10,000 hours of original tapes that predated the archival recording were also made available.

All of this content is easily accessible online through the C-SPAN Video Library. Programs are indexed by the date that they occurred as well as when they aired. The latter helps with creating a schedule and retrieving programs, but it is the event date that is the important historical date. The following are identified for each program: a title, category, and format; the organization that sponsored the event (hosting organization); a brief description of what occurred; the name, title, and affiliation of all who appear. Those affiliations are also used to designate with the hosting organization so that one can differentiate between an organization that sponsors an event and the people from that organization who appear in that event. A set of nested keywords is also attached to each program.

A typical record looks like this:

Format: Speech
Title: Unemployment Insurance Extension
Organizer: White House
Event Date: January 7, 2014
Summary: President Obama urged Congress to pass a bill to extend emergency unemployment benefits. His remarks came after the Senate voted to advance the bill.
Person-Title-Affiliation: Barack Obama, President, U.S.
Tags: Business and Commerce — Employment Policy — Unemployment
Advanced an unemployment benefits extension bill that would extend insurance for eligible workers for 3 months.

Since 1992, C-SPAN has been capturing digital closed captioning text that is time stamped with the time that it was recorded. These captions enable text based searching to find video clips. Closed captioning for U.S. House and Senate sessions has existed the longest and is the most developed. Because the House and Senate caption their own sessions and identify each speaker, we are able to match these speaker names with our database, create a chronological index of all congressional speakers, and link these appearances to the

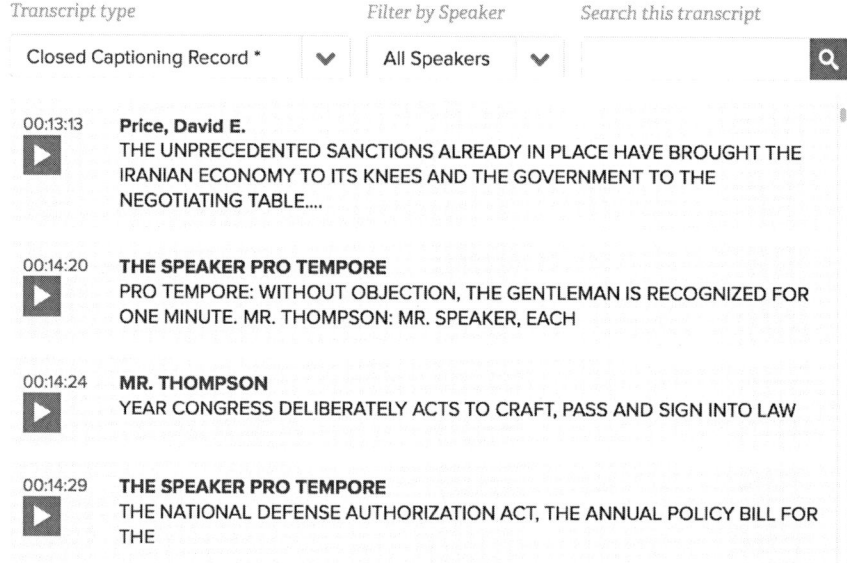

Figure 2.1 An example of the searchable closed captioning record for a House session. (© 2014 by C-SPAN.)

text of their remarks. Furthermore, we are able to link the closed captioned text to the *Congressional Record,* the official record of their remarks. Since members are allowed to change their remarks and to insert remarks into the record that were never made, the C-SPAN recording becomes an invaluable research tool and the real record of what transpires on the House and Senate floors. (See Figure 2.1.)

Using computer records of C-SPAN's productions, we are able to create the same time-based index of most C-SPAN programs, including congressional hearings. These records allow the creation of within-program speaker indexes that allow users to search by speaker or by words within individual programs. A typical index is shown in Figure 2.2.

The indexing system allows searching across programs by any of the indexed terms, including the closed caption text. For presidential events the official transcript is attached and time indexed. So for all presidential events, an actual transcript can be searched to find the video reference. (See Figure 2.3.)

The Video Library permits clipping and sharing of video. These clips make it easy for users to select just a portion of a longer video to illustrate a

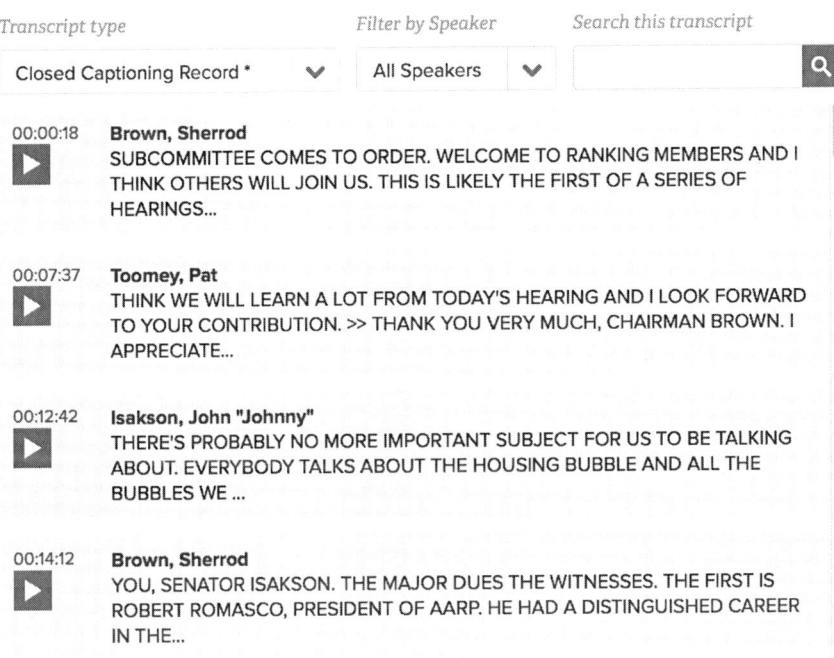

Figure 2.2 The searchable closed captioning record for a congressional hearing. (© 2014 by C-SPAN.)

comment or statement that they want to emphasize by simply moving the begin and end point selectors to select the portion of the video they want to clip. These clips remain on the C-SPAN servers, and all have a permanent link so that they can be used repeatedly. The links can be shared, and many videos can be embedded in blogs or Web pages. By creating a MyC-SPAN account,

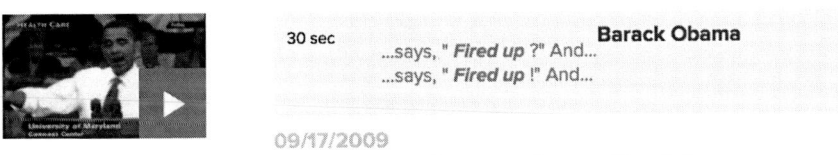

Figure 2.3 The transcript record of a portion of a presidential speech. (© 2014 by C-SPAN.)

users can keep a directory of all of their clips and return to their personal account to retrieve or share these clips. Creating and sharing video clips is an effective use of the Video Library.

All of this indexing and text linking, as well as its software systems, make the C-SPAN Video Library an unparalleled resource for communication, political science, historical, and sociological research. In this volume, 12 scholars present applications from teaching, research, and engagement that utilize the Video Library. It is hoped that these scholars inspire others to extend their applications in new and enhanced ways. This volume is simply a first step—a guide to the possible, to the "what ifs" of teaching, research, and engagement.

This volume contains four examples of how C-SPAN can be used in teaching and six examples of C-SPAN use in communication research. Each of the contributors is an insightful innovator. All are leaders in their fields who are either exploring ways to use primary source video to introduce students to process and concepts or introducing new research horizons that they examine through data collected from video. This volume contains other essays as well—those that explore community outreach, insights into C-SPAN, and the challenge of incivility in public discourse.

Chapter 3 contains reflective comments by C-SPAN founder and executive chairman Brian Lamb. He talks about the early days of C-SPAN, its unique place in the media world through its funding model, its mission, and its commitment to providing balanced coverage of public affairs through editorial and production values.

Following Brian Lamb's remarks, scholars with different approaches to research in communication present ways that C-SPAN can be used in research. In Chapter 4, Professor Theon Hill of Wheaton College presents a thought-provoking look at political rhetoric of the first Black president and the interpretations that can be made in light of the legacy of African American rhetorical styles. In Chapter 5, a historical approach is taken by Professor Kathryn Cramer Brownell, who reaches back into the Archives to study the 1984 presidential campaign, with particular attention to how C-SPAN call-in programs can reveal underlying opinion that differs from popular perception. Brownell's research demonstrates the value of the Archives to a historian looking back 30 years in time.

In Chapter 6, Professor Colene Lind, a communication scholar, takes us forward in time to the 2010 period to look at the interaction of citizens and their elected officials in congressional town hall meetings. The character of these interactions is explored using video recordings of these town meetings from the C-SPAN Video Library. In Chapter 7, a different approach is taken by Professor Stephanie Bor, who explores the use of social media by C-SPAN to promote its mission and the awareness of the C-SPAN Video Library.

Christopher Kowal (Chapter 8) and Sorin Matei (Chapter 9) both push the limits of current research by using innovative techniques to develop new data from the video record. Professor Matei looks at the patterns of interactions of individuals in committee hearings. Rather than just looking at who speaks the most, he examines the how people follow and respond to each other in their remarks. The result is a diagram that creates network relationships that can demonstrate new perspectives on the importance of certain individuals in the social situation. His work is in the tradition of analysis of "big data."

Professor Kowal's work illustrates the importance of the underlying concept of emotion in speeches. By using facial recognition technology, he introduces us to the concept of emotion and how it can be observed and measured through detection software to add a totally new but vital dimension to analysis of candidate remarks. The possibilities that Kowal's research offers to the study of politicians and candidates may motivate a wide range of research.

Following these research presentations, we turn to four teaching presentations by professors who use C-SPAN video to introduce ideas in the classroom. In Chapter 10, Professor Glenn Sparks describes three examples from his Theories of Mass Communication class that use C-SPAN Video Library clips to expose students to theorists and their ideas. In Chapter 11, I provide two examples from political science that have relevance to communication as well, and in Chapter 12, I describe some distance learning and the Purdue Institute for Civic Communication (PICC) initiatives from Purdue that are innovative ways of using C-SPAN video. Finally, in Chapter 13, William Oakes and his engineering colleagues explain the outreach that they achieve in their Engineering Programs in the Community (EPICS). This program demonstrates the value of engagement as a direction for other universities.

In a capstone essay that is the first C-SPAN Archives Distinguished Lecture (Chapter 14), Professor Roderick Hart reflects on his mother's love of C-SPAN, the need for engagement for our political system to function, and why incivility is an insidious force for the body politic. His essay reflects on the importance of C-SPAN to civil communication and a functioning political system.

These collective essays all draw on C-SPAN and its Video Library to demonstrate the value of this extensive indexed public affairs video collection for research, teaching, and engagement. Without the founding of the Archives and the decision to record, index, preserve, and now digitally distribute C-SPAN programming, none of this would be possible, or it would be very difficult to obtain the video. Now we are at the beginning of a new era as, Susan Swain reminds us in Chapter 1. These scholars have just taken the first step. We expect to see more development from each of them and, more importantly, we want to encourage many other professors to pursue the lines of research highlighted here, as well as forge paths with new insightful research, teaching, and engagement.

The C-SPAN Video Library provides the content and the tools to enable that research. Just as the network leaves it to the viewers to form their own opinions on its programming, by extension the C-SPAN Video Library does the same. It encourages the faculty and students to form their own research questions, to mine the C-SPAN Video Library to find the clips and the data to answer their own research questions, and to encourage others to follow in their footprints. Let the research begin.

CHAPTER 3

C-SPAN'S ORIGINS AND PLACE IN HISTORY: PERSONAL COMMENTARY

Brian Lamb, Founder and Executive Chairperson, C-SPAN

In this informal luncheon address, Brian Lamb touches on a number of points of interest to scholars and viewers of C-SPAN. This essay provides anecdotes about C-SPAN's origins and distinctive nature, as well as about its place in media history and contemporary political discussions. These comments center around several themes: (1) in the beginning . . ., (2) C-SPAN's nature and impact, (3) access to C-SPAN content, (4) media maneuverings from an insider's view, and (5) C-SPAN's future.

IN THE BEGINNING . . .

Dr. Robert Browning has already provided some good background on the C-SPAN Archives and information about C-SPAN. I don't want to be redundant, so I'll just tell you this: the most important thing for you to know about C-SPAN is that it was created by individuals; there's no money in it from the government—it's completely a private industry effort. A cable entrepreneur named Bob Rosencrans wrote the first check to fund C-SPAN back in 1978. He is now 87 years old and lives in Connecticut. His business partner was Kenneth Gunter, who recently passed away at age 80 and lived in San Angelo, Texas.

In several ways, these two men represent what this company is all about. Bob Rosecrans is short, bald, Jewish, and liberal. Ken Gunter was tall, had a full head of hair, was Presbyterian, and was a former "John Bircher." One lives in Connecticut; one lived in Texas. The two of them were in the cable television business together for many years and they were incredibly successful. They were the first ones back in 1977 to say, "We think what you want to do with C-SPAN is worth doing. We'll get behind it and we'll write you a check." It wasn't a big check, it was worth $25,000, but their names were big within the early cable television industry and it opened the doors for the rest of the seed money that we needed to start C-SPAN.

In all, we raised about $450,000, which for me, coming from Lafayette, Indiana, where my father was a small businessman, was a lot of money. In the television business, it's nothing. Even today our institution, which spends about $65 million a year, spends nothing compared, for instance, to either MSNBC or Fox News. Fox News last year made over a billion dollars; they didn't gross a billion, they *made* over a billion dollars. By comparison, we took in and spent about $65 million. We can do this because our mission is very simple: we want the public to be able to see what goes on in their government and in their political system, by showing events in their entirety and then allowing viewers to make up their own minds about what happens in Washington.

C-SPAN'S NATURE AND IMPACT

This kind of reality television is not everybody's cup of tea. In fact, we don't actually know how many people watch our networks. In 2013, *The New York Times* thought they had figured out our ratings. They weren't being conniving, but they found somebody who could read a ratings book and wrote a story about it. When we saw their report on our numbers it was a little concerning because they weren't very big for a single day, but they did indicate 9 million viewers tuning in over the course of a month.

Of course, you have to look at these audience numbers with some perspective: How much do you spend to get the audience you have? ESPN, for instance, gets $5.50 to $7.00 a month per customer who subscribes to cable or satellite television. C-SPAN gets six cents. If you've never looked at television audience numbers, ESPN is generally the number one cable channel. In a typical week, it might have somewhere around 3 million viewers. Fox News is the second most-watched cable channel with about 2 million per week, so you can see that even for the big cable networks, the audiences are relatively small in a country that has over 300 million people. And when you look at the audience numbers, you also have to look at the money spent to produce and market the channels. The more money you have, the more pizzazz you have, the more stars you have, and the bigger your audience.

C-SPAN has been able to fit into this world because when we started back in 1979, there wasn't much available on cable television. There are now about three or four hundred cable channels, but when we started, we were just the sixth network to launch. The first one was HBO. Right up in that early group also was Showtime, a direct copy of HBO. One that everybody misses when they talk about the early days of cable television is WYAH, Channel 27 in Portsmouth, Virginia. The YAH stands for "Yahweh," and the channel belonged to Pat Robertson. He was able to figure out a way to get his network up on a satellite and called it the Christian Broadcasting Network.

C-SPAN was there early, or we wouldn't exist today. Intentionally, we have no ratings, we have no stars. Importantly, we have no advertising. That means we have just one stream of revenue—the fees paid by our affiliates for carrying C-SPAN. We're not sure in the next 25 years how long that framework can last. The cable industry is at the point where the Internet is making a difference in its financial structure. It hasn't changed the economics of the business yet, because along the way, the cable companies added telephone service and Internet to their video packages. Most of them will tell you that these days, their video subscriptions break even at best, and their telephone and Internet businesses are where they make a lot of their money, and also in advertising. So C-SPAN is sitting in the middle off all this dynamic change in the industry, holding on for dear life.

Diminishing the power of the network television executives in New York was my objective when I first got into cable television. Before cable came along, the networks were the only channels Americans could watch, and they just had too much power. Today, they are still making lots of money, but because of cable and satellite, no one has the kind of power that they used to have when I was growing up back in the '60s. As an example, *60 Minutes* used to bring CBS about 30 to 40 million viewers on Sunday nights; today it has about 12 million viewers.

C-SPAN started about 16 or 17 months before CNN did; most people don't know that. We started on March 19, 1979, and they started on June 1, 1980. I knew a lot of the folks over at CNN when they started, and in the beginning they were a little frustrated with us. Because we were so different, we got a lot of initial publicity, and they couldn't figure out why this little network was getting the publicity, and they weren't. The mainstream news media made fun of them in the beginning as well, calling them the "Chicken Noodle Network," which was really not fair.

Ted Turner was a lot of things, but more than anything else, he loved clobbering competitors. We were not competing for his audience but we were competing for space on cable systems, and when we both started, some cable systems were only 20 channels. I remember well when Ted Turner went to Indianapolis on March 30, 1981, and said before an audience of cable television operators, "Take C-SPAN off and put us on"—and he meant this kind of thing. So we had a very competitive relationship in the very beginning. Certain individuals at CNN were somewhat helpful, but the hierarchy didn't want anything to do with helping us in the early days. However, as the years went by, we developed a good relationship with them. By the way, don't feel sorry for CNN. Today, even with all the competition in their marketplace, CNN made $600 million last year. Their ratings aren't as high as Fox, but they are really two different institutions. But all three—CNN, Fox, and MSNBC—they're all battling for that same cable news audience. Today we have a desk-to-desk relationship that gets above the business issues. We help them, they help us—we trade event coverage back and forth.

Speaking of change and C-SPAN's distinctive nature, one aspect of C-SPAN that hasn't changed over the years is our approach to our on-camera staff. We established this place with no stars—on purpose. Unlike every other network, we don't promote our on-air people as personalities. Now, this is and it isn't about the money. What drove the philosophy was having a place in news and public affairs television where it wasn't about the stars but about the information. I watch a lot of television news and I know and like a lot of their on-camera people, but it's gotten way out of control. If you take the four anchor people at the four biggest networks, their salaries would constitute much of C-SPAN's budget for a year. The system is out of whack. I don't mean to offend people who are making $12 million a year as an anchor, but it's crazy. There is so much money in the business; it changes how you think.

When someone comes to work at C-SPAN every day they never think, "How can we focus on something that will get us a bigger audience?" If you work at any of the other institutions, that is the first thing you have to think about. That's why you see the cable networks get into this serial coverage of one event that goes on for a week or more. I'm not really being critical of them; they can do whatever they want to do. But I believe the star system has changed the whole nature of the news. Why do they send a guy all the way to the Philippines to stand amongst the rubble of a tsunami for days on end, doing personal stories? Not because we learn a lot from it, but because it brings in viewers. They fly them over there in private jets. They fly in their equipment and they're in business. They don't even think about it when they do it; it's just the way it works. You look around, not so much for the most impactful news, but for the best people stories because if viewers are watching you then you can sell eyeballs to advertisers. It's just the way it is. As viewers, we only have ourselves to blame if we don't like what we see on television. So far, enough people are watching this kind of thing to keep it all going just as it is.

ACCESS TO C-SPAN CONTENT

We are incredibly grateful to Robert Browning, who devised the programming archive that is based in West Layette, Indiana. Nobody has ever done anything like what we are doing with the C-SPAN Archives, especially providing the public the opportunity to watch over 200,000 hours of searchable video via the Internet, all for free. Through the years, the members of our board, who are all cable television executives, have always been open and generous in making our content widely available. They have never really wanted to hoard what they paid to create in C-SPAN. With their blessing, we provided the C-SPAN channels to the satellite TV companies even before the government mandated it. And, today, satellite distributors make up 35% of our affiliate base.

Another credit to our funders—they have never interfered with us editorially. We've never had board members call us up and say, "Cover this," or "Don't televise that." In the early days, we occasionally had a few individuals get a little scrappy in this regard. When they did, I went to the chairman of our board and said, "We've got some guy demanding that we cover this or that." His immediate response was to put an amendment in our corporate bylaws declaring that no board member has the right to say anything about programming content. But the reality is, we've just never had a real problem with editorial pressure from our funders. As consumers get more and more media choices, we'll have less of this kind of interference anywhere in the journalism business, because there's going to be less and less power in any one content provider's hands.

MEDIA MANEUVERINGS FROM AN INSIDER'S VIEW

Congressional hearings are C-SPAN's bread and butter, and there is a very strange policy on Capitol Hill which is mind-boggling to me: if a television network decides it wants more than one camera in a hearing room, as we always do, then you have to make your video available to all accredited news organizations—for free. This means that every time you watch any of the news programs and you see testimony from Capitol Hill, those are likely C-SPAN cameras, and that material was given to every network for free. It makes no sense at all. After years and years of getting millions of dollars of free video from us, an individual at one of the commercial networks, ABC, agreed with our complaints about this and said that, going forward, their network pool would provide us with the president's video wherever he appeared domestically. We don't have the money to send a producer running after the president, which is very expensive. So now, at least, there's something of a trade-off. There has been a lot of stuff like this that's gone on over the years; sometimes people in our business would say, "We'll be glad to help you, just don't tell anybody."

The first person in the commercial networks to come along and really be helpful to C-SPAN was Tim Russert, the now-deceased host of *Meet the Press*. Tim had come out of Congress; he had worked for New York Senator Pat Moynihan and then New York Governor Mario Cuomo, and he appreciated what we were trying to do. I remember picking up the paper one day during the 1984 conventions and the *Washington Post* had done an article on us. They quoted a very favorable comment from some guy named Tim Russert. I didn't know him and ultimately first met him, I think, in Dallas at the GOP convention. He could not have been more pleasant or more interested in helping us. He and I had a great relationship. We weren't close friends, but we had many a hallway conversation. He was frequently a guest on the C-SPAN programs that I hosted, and he had me on his shows.

Together, Tim Russert and I got something done by working on a very human level back in 1997. That's the year that C-SPAN successfully bid on a noncommercial radio station license here in Washington, DC. While growing up in Lafayette, Indiana, I worked at WASK Radio for five years. I always loved radio and I still love radio more than anything. So, when we got this radio station here in the local area, I picked up the phone and called Tim, and I said, "I have this crazy idea. What would you think of letting us have the audio of your *Meet the Press* shows on Sunday to put on our radio station later that day?" He called me back about a week later and said, "You've got a deal." And then he said something that you'll get a kick out of: Tim was a law school grad, but he said, "Let's not go to the lawyers. If we go to the lawyers, we'll never get this job done." He said, "You send me a letter and I'll send you a letter and we'll just agree to do it." I think he was right: if the network bosses had gotten into this discussion, we'd never have had the deal. Once we had agreed, and I told Tim I was going to do this, I picked up the phone and called Cokie Roberts at ABC, Bob Schieffer at CBS, Tony Snow at Fox, and Wolf Blitzer at CNN and said, "Tim Russert just agreed to put *Meet the Press* on C-SPAN Radio on Sundays. How about you letting us have *This Week* on ABC? . . ." Every single one of them said yes. A lot of that sort of person-to-person exchange happens in this business and re-airing the networks' Sunday show lineup has been a real public service in this town.

A major challenge that C-SPAN and others in this business will have to deal with in the years ahead will be the politicians themselves. Politicians love control. They love to control their own image, and as they do more of that, they can make doing business difficult for us. As television has gotten more and more dominant, politicians have gotten more involved in trying to control what the public sees of them. I'll give you an example: The cameras that cover the floor of the House and the Senate belong to those two institutions—they control them. We have proposed to every party that's ever taken control of the House or the Senate that they allow us to put our own cameras in their chambers. We proposed this to Speaker Gingrich as he took office in 1995; I wrote a letter to him and said "We'd like to put our own cameras in there." He immediately said, "That sounds like a very good idea, let's talk about it." That initial reaction is generally the last time you hear an elected official say anything positive about private camera coverage of Congress.

Bob Dole, as Majority Leader of the Senate, said to us, "Hey, that's a great idea!" We never heard from him again. Not a word. No meetings, nothing. The House did set up a committee to study our request. The reason they did that, of course, was that they had no intention of ever allowing our cameras into their chamber. But, they started this committee and had a Republican and a Democrat leading it. We met with them and after several meetings, you begin to understand that it's not going anywhere. In the midst of some serious discussions with them about how we could we get this done, one of the congressmen said, "We've got an idea, and we want to know what you think of it: How about we rope off an area at the back of the House of Representatives, and if we want to deal with each other, we'll go inside that rope line and you all will agree not to show that."

When you're a journalist, your immediate reaction is to say, "Are you crazy?" You'd have to tell the audience, "By the way folks, in the House chamber at this moment they're all huddled over behind that rope line making their deals but we can't show you that." Now, I'll tell you why they wanted this sequestered location: Some of you may remember the vote on the prescription drug bill. The Republicans didn't have the votes they needed and they held the vote open for three hours in the middle of the night trying to get those final votes. Cabinet officers were on the floor of the House, corralling members. Tommy Thompson, then the head of Health and Human Services, was one of them, going around the floor, trying to get that last vote. We televised it, of course, for the full three hours, without commentary. News organizations figured it out after the fact; they found Thompson in the video and put a graphic around him and demonstrated him making his way around the floor. That roped-off area in the House chamber for deal making would have prevented this kind of high stakes, last-minute lobbying from ever going public.

If you were up close to these institutions and watched how often they try, all parties, to keep the public from seeing exactly what's going on in this town, it might fry you. Political fundraisers are important examples of this. These are big dinners; 800 to 1,000 people at public events at big hotels and there are always lots of donors sitting around the tables. The organizers will say, "Okay, you can have one camera, but you're going to have to put it in the back of the room." They don't really want us showing who's sitting at these tables, even though under the law they have to disclose who their donors are and how much money they are contributing to the parties.

I do understand the pushback from politicians, because when you stand up in front of a group and see cameras focusing on you, you're conscious of it. You are thinking, "That video could keep what I'm saying here alive forever"; and it often does. So you can't really blame politicians for trying to control their environment. But they are public officials and they do work for the public, which has a right to see what happens here.

One of the things I've seen change over the last 46 years in the coverage of Washington is a by-product of the increased competition in news. Today, there's so much competition to get an interview, say, with the president that news organizations find out that if they aren't "behaving themselves," the president's people could easily say, "You can't have an interview. You're not cooperating with us; we're not going to cooperate with you." It happens—trust me. It's a struggle all the time between government and the news media. It even happens to C-SPAN, believe it or not.

Then there is the question of access to the Supreme Court. First of all, let me say up front: the Supreme Court is a tremendous institution. Of all three branches of government, it's the best run, and it's the most impressive up close. It's also a small organization. There are only about 350 people working in that beautiful building built in 1935 by William Howard Taft. Twenty-five years ago I remember saying in an interview, "We'll be in the Court with our cameras in 5 years." Well, as you can see, that didn't happen. There is a real aversion to television on the part of the Supreme Court. There is no one reason that they'll give you. I've always thought that the real reason, if you got below the surface arguments, is that they don't want to end up as sound bites on Jon Stewart's *Daily Show*. The reality is, they end up there anyway. His producers use a still photo and the audio. Jon Stewart doesn't have a problem making fun of anybody when he wants to. But, I think they just want to avoid that ability for people to grab a sound bite. Over the years, we have made every argument on behalf of television. We say to them, "Why should you give the benefit to a reporter who's got a pencil in their hand to come into the Court and quote you, but not television cameras? Why do you allow somebody who uses crayons or chalk to come in and make the sketches of the arguments, but cameras are excluded?" Clearly, these arguments haven't prevailed.

This being said, the Court has been very good to us, overall. We did a documentary on them and all of the justices talked to us on the record and several of them even opened up their private chambers to our cameras. My colleague Susan Swain and I each did half of the interviews: together, we interviewed all 11 of the living justices. It was a really good experience. We agreed going into this project that we were not going to ask them in these interviews about television coverage of the Court. They were willing to let us in, so we thought it wasn't appropriate to use these interviews as a platform to lobby for cameras. But we have asked them individually on other programs. For example, I have an interview program that airs on Sunday nights and I've had Stephen Breyer, John Paul Stevens, Antonin Scalia, and Clarence Thomas all on the program. The reason they will come on, usually, is because they have a book out. I did four interviews—it was just an unbelievable experience—with Chief Justice William Rehnquist. He didn't like to be interviewed, and the only reason I got these interviews was that he had a book out and he agreed to come on and talk about the book. One of these interviews occurred when he was about ready to preside in the United States Senate during the Clinton impeachment process. I was interviewing him about one of his books, which was about the impeachment attempt on Samuel Chase, who was on the Supreme Court. I said to myself, "I'm going to see if I can get him to comment on his involvement in the Clinton impeachment through this historic story." I no more than got the words out of my mouth when he said, "Nope, not going to do that; not going there." He very much controlled what he was willing to talk about.

When it comes to putting television cameras in the courtroom, individual justices have been all over the lot. Ultimately, what it gets down to is that in order to have it happen, all nine of them are going to have to put up their hands and say yes. . . . I now believe we're not going to get there for a long time—not until there is a leader of the Court who convinces the other Justices that a primary reason to do it is for public education.

You may not realize this, but they are only in oral arguments about 75 hours a year. And in spite of what any of them say, my guess is that very few times do the Justices ever change their opinions based on oral arguments. They make their decision based on the briefs that are filed in these cases. But, the Court is hung up on television coverage right now. There is another thing I am sure they say to themselves: "Why should we mess with this fabulous institution? Why should we take a chance? It's respected." It has gotten, in the view of some people, more political in the last few years, but it's still more respected than the other institutions in Washington. So, they say, "Why take a chance?" We would argue, "Only one reason: That the judicial branch of government is so darned important that if it wasn't for one vote of one single Justice, for example, the heath care law would be toast." They are public servants, and it seems to me, the Court is so powerful that the public has a right, especially in this new age of nonintrusive technology, to see it. Yes, they have been nominated and confirmed for life by the United States Senate, but the media plays an important role in a democracy like ours; and in spite of the fact the Court might not always like the outcome of coverage, it really is a significant part of this system. It's hard though, once you're sitting on the Court, to vote for change.

C-SPAN'S FUTURE

C-SPAN celebrated its 35th anniversary in 2014. Steve Scully, our senior executive producer, has been here for 22 years; Susan Swain, our co-CEO, has been here for 32 years. They and their colleagues are as much a part of our mission as I am. I got to come along in the beginning with an idea that, by the way, was initially rejected. I probably had a hundred nos before I got a yes. Even after I got that yes from Bob Rosencrans, a month after we got into it he called me and said, "We've decided not to do it." Then, the idea came up of televising the House, and everybody got on board. But the people who work here are every bit as much in favor of what C-SPAN is doing as I am. That's the legacy.

Frequently, we go around our company and try to change the way we do things, and people will say, "Whoa! Wait a minute, C-SPAN doesn't do things that way." People who work at our network are invested in our mission, and that will preserve our legacy, too. The only thing that will substantially change us, and believe me it will change us, is if our revenues go down the drain; if, all of a sudden, the model changes and our affiliates say, "We're not going to support you anymore." You can see that going on all over the place in the media right now; there is so much change. We're trying to figure it out. We talk about this a lot: How does C-SPAN survive if everything dramatically changes? Do we go to advertising? Do we increase our rates? We don't have answers yet. Even though I'm no longer the CEO, I want to hang around for a little bit longer, and I'm hoping that I don't have to see that kind of fundamental change to our structure. But we do think about it a lot. If we want C-SPAN to be around for the long haul, we can't have our heads in the sand about the future.

PART II

RESEARCH CASE STUDIES USING RHETORICAL AND HISTORICAL LENSES

CHAPTER 4

PRESERVING BLACK POLITICAL AGENCY IN THE AGE OF OBAMA: UTILIZING THE C-SPAN VIDEO ARCHIVES IN RHETORICAL SCHOLARSHIP

Theon E. Hill, Wheaton College

Barack Obama's historic election as the 44th president of the United States of America generated tremendous optimism in the Black community that social change was possible. His status as the first Black president attracted unprecedented levels of support in the Black community (Ansolabehere & Stewart III, 2009; Balz & Cohen, 2007). The promise of the age of Obama led some to identify him as a contemporary Moses who would lead African Americans into the Promised Land of freedom and equality (Drash, 2009, para. 7). Obama, according to this perspective, was the anointed leader destined to complete the journey started by Martin Luther King Jr. His emergence inaugurated a new age of Black political agency, one in which the dream would become reality. In this chapter, I use the phrase *Black political agency* to refer to the means by which African Americans advocated for various causes and policies impacting their community. For example, the exercise of political agency could consist of marching in support of a cause or delivering a speech in support of a cause or policy. Despite the optimism surrounding Obama's presidency, many issues facing the Black community persisted and, in some cases, even worsened during his first few years in office. The combination of tremendous support for the president and unaddressed issues in the Black community created a situation in which some Black leaders felt constrained in their ability to advocate for policies benefitting the Black community.

In this chapter, I draw on the C-SPAN Video Library (http://www.c-span.org) to examine the nature of the challenges that Black leaders perceived in the age of Obama and how they sought to navigate these challenges. I focus my brief rhetorical analysis of the comments of Georgetown professor Michael Eric Dyson at Tavis Smiley's (2010) forum, "We Count! The Black Agenda is the American Agenda." Dyson's comments offer key insight into the ways that certain Black leaders sought to preserve political agency in the age of Obama. By offering complete access to important texts, the C-SPAN Archives serves as a strategic resource for this study and, in a broader sense, for my entire research agenda focusing on rhetoric and social change. The C-SPAN Archives offers access to a wide variety of texts such as this one in which the relationship between rhetoric and social change becomes central. The coverage that C-SPAN gives to issues such as Black political agency in the age of Obama is not mirrored by any other network, including networks focused on African American concerns such as BET. Much of my research focuses on the role of radical or fringe rhetoric in pursuing social change. Without C-SPAN's commitment to covering vital social issues from divergent perspectives, my research would be severely handicapped. The video footage of Smiley's event allows me to engage perspectives and opinions that typically go uncovered by other media outlets. Apart from in-person attendance, studying the rhetoric at events like Smiley's would be extremely difficult. The analysis that follows consists of a rhetorical analysis of Michael Eric Dyson's comments at Tavis Smiley's forum that is available through the Archives (see Figure 4.1). Prior to my analysis, I will first situate this essay within the historical context in which Smiley's forum occurred.

Figure 4.1 Georgetown professor Michael Eric Dyson was one of many African American leaders disappointed with President Obama's reluctance to target issues facing Black America. (From Smiley, 2010. © 2010 by C-SPAN.)

BACKGROUND: BLACK DISCONTENT IN THE AGE OF OBAMA

When Obama took office, the nation was reeling from a devastating economic recession, soaring health care costs, and two wars. Rising unemployment levels crippled families across the nation. Building on the work of his predecessor, Obama moved swiftly to address America's economic woes. His efforts materialized in the American Reinvestment and Recovery Act, a stimulus bill designed to alleviate the financial pain that many Americans were feeling. In the months following the passage of the $787 billion stimulus bill, studies revealed that the bill failed to address the disproportionate levels of poverty and unemployment in minority communities (Padgett, 2009). While the stimulus contributed to an initial slight decline in national unemployment levels, job loss rates in African American and Hispanic communities continued to rise steadily (Kirwan Institute, 2010b). Researchers found that stimulus money was not being directed to those communities hit hardest by the recession (Kirwan Institute, 2010a). The failure of the government to effectively address disparities in minority communities contributed to national poverty rates that were actually higher than rates during the civil rights movement (Tough, 2012). These alarming statistics caused many Black leaders to question the adequacy of Obama's policies to eliminate inequality in the Black community (Padgett, 2009).

Initially, Obama's status as the nation's first Black president shielded his administration from criticisms for a lack of progress on combating inequality in the African American community. Those who dared to raise concerns with Obama's policies were met with fierce opposition (Terry, 2010). Supporters of the president called on the discontent to be patient (Hutchinson, 2010). Obama, his supporters argued, encountered daily opposition to his agenda from Republicans and an increasingly vocal Tea Party. What he needed most from African Americans was support and protection from those seeking to derail his agenda. African Americans had invested a great deal of hope in Obama's ability to lead them to the Promised Land (Drash, 2009). This investment led to what some began to call Obama's "racial pass" (Hutchinson, 2010). That is, many African Americans trusted Obama so much that they did not see the need to hold him accountable for his exercise of power. His presence in the White House was sufficient to merit the support of the community. For two centuries, the prophetic tradition of speaking truth to power was the foundation of Black political agency (Chappell, 2005; Raboteau, 1994; West, 1993, 2002). Now, the advent of the first Black president complicated efforts to complete the journey to the Promised Land.

News of the failure of the stimulus to effectively combat the severe effects of the recession in the Black community revived the complaints of Obama's critics (Terry, 2010; Tough, 2012). Activists, intellectuals, and even members of the Congressional Black Caucus demanded that the Obama administration do more to deal with economic disparities by submitting legislation designed to create jobs in minority communities (Cooper, 2010; National Public Radio, 2010). At the heart of their complaints and demands was the belief that current policies did not sufficiently address structural inequalities. The disproportionate levels of poverty, they argued, required specific policies to address the unique needs of the Black community. In their opinion, the president needed a "Black agenda" (Terry, 2010). Obama faced what *New York Times* writer Sheryl Stolberg (2010, para. 4) called "a balancing act." The challenge of this act was to satisfy multiple constituencies without appearing to privilege any.

Differences over the adequacy of Obama's policy agenda generated numerous debates among Black leaders. The debates culminated in a heated exchange between Tavis Smiley and Al Sharpton on Sharpton's radio show in February of 2010. Sharpton had been quoted in *The New York Times* as saying that the president was "smart not to ballyhoo 'a black agenda'" (Stolberg, 2010, para. 15). Smiley took this statement as evidence that certain Black leaders were giving the president a pass on issues facing the community. When the topic came up on Sharpton's radio show, the two argued over the need for Obama to have a "Black agenda" and whether or not the president's Black supporters, such as Sharpton, were failing to hold him accountable for his policies.

The central issue driving this debate concerned the appropriate mode of Black political agency in the age of Obama. The prophetic mode of political engagement seen during the civil rights movement (Chappell, 2005; Rustin, 1965) was threatened by a president who was viewed as both a prophetic leader and a political figure. That is, leaders wrestled with how to speak truth to power when a Black president who was frequently linked to King and Moses occupied the seat of power (Drash, 2009; Gitell, 2008; F. C. Harris, 2012). In light of the "long-simmering debate," Smiley organized the forum "We Count! The Black Agenda is the American Agenda" on March 20, 2010, at Chicago State University to discuss the need for and form of a Black agenda (Wickham, 2010, para. 1). Given the president's popularity in the Black community, the forum attracted criticism for Smiley and the other participants (Chicago Defender, 2010; Coley, 2010; H. R. Harris, 2010). The president's supporters argued that the criticisms were unproductive at a time when Obama was fighting conservatives on health care reform. According to the president's supporters, challenging the president's policy agenda advanced the agenda of the political right. Smiley and other critics were cast as disloyal traitors motived by envy and bitterness.

WE COUNT! DEMANDS FOR A BLACK AGENDA

Smiley's forum featured 11 panelists, including religious leaders (Louis Farrakhan and Jesse Jackson), public intellectuals (Michael Eric Dyson, Michael Fauntroy, Julianne Malveaux, Ronald Walters, and Cornel West), corporate CEOs (Angela Glover Blackwell and Tom Burrell), a politician (Dorothy Tillman), and a

Figure 4.2 Dyson joined 10 other panelists at Smiley's forum, including the Rev. Jesse Jackson, Dr. Cornel West, and Minister Louis Farrakhan. (From Smiley, 2010. © 2010 by C-SPAN.)

Chicago State University undergraduate student (Raven Curling) (see Figure 4.2). The event lasted approximately three hours and featured a lively discussion on whether or not the president needed a Black agenda, what that agenda should look like, and the nature of Black political agency in the age of Obama. At the forum, the panelists sought to defend their insistence that a Black agenda was needed with the idea that such an agenda served the best interests of the entire nation. They sought to restore Black political agency where they perceived it had been lost. Finally, they expressed love and support for the president in the face of strong opposition and even death threats. Midway through the conversation, Smiley (2010) turned the conversation to Georgetown professor Michael Eric Dyson with the question, "What about the question that Obama is the first Black president . . . and there is only so far down the field that he can push the ball? Maybe our expectations of him are unreasonable." Dyson's response to this question offers a perspective on what Black political agency looks like in the age of Obama. To highlight this perspective, I will draw on aspects of the original Exodus narrative from the Old Testament to unpack some of Dyson's biblically grounded comments. In his comments, Dyson articulated several metaphoric relationships from The Exodus that he perceived in African American discussions about Obama, his significance, and his policy agenda. In my analysis, I argue that Michael Eric Dyson's metaphoric use of The Exodus narrative at the event suggests that African Americans must adopt a critical stance toward Obama as a means of preserving their political agency in the 21st century.

OBAMA AS MOSES

In his response to Smiley's question, Dyson expressed his belief that African Americans have misunderstood the importance of Obama's historic election: "You think Obama is Moses." To Dyson, the common assumption in the African American community "Obama is Moses" was dangerous because it prevented African Americans from holding him accountable for the policies that he advanced and their impact on various communities. His statement is loaded with assumptions. Dyson's use of the metaphor *Obama is Moses* highlights how Obama sought to position himself in the Black imagination as a deliverer in the prophetic tradition and how African Americans received him. Both Obama's rhetorical practices and African American reception/perception evidence a perspective of Obama as a prophetic deliverer (Drash, 2009; Murphy, 2011).

In the biblical Exodus, Moses, God's prophet, challenged Pharaoh's authority out of obedience to a higher power. To put it more clearly, prophetic authority functioned to hold political authority accountable. Political authority received power from the people, while prophetic authority received power from God. The position that Obama occupied as a contemporary deliverer in the mold of Moses or Martin Luther King Jr. rendered African Americans unable to exercise their political agency to advocate for causes important to the community. As a prophet, Obama was immune to criticism. In ancient Israel, prophets spoke as God's representatives among the people (Baker, 1996).

Throughout the journey to the Promised Land, Moses faced multiple challenges to his leadership from a variety of leaders in Israel. By highlighting the fact that African Americans held Obama to be a contemporary Moses, Dyson situated Obama as the natural recipient of criticism as a part of his prophetic office. However, Dyson also implied that this persona shields Obama from these criticisms and delegitimizes those who would seek to hold the president accountable for the policies that he advances. That is, metaphoric linkages of

Obama to Moses wedded the prophetic and political in a way that marginalized the political agency of African Americans to critique the president. To criticize one of God's prophets was to incur the wrath of God.

Like all authentic Old Testament prophets, Moses's calling was divine in origin (Baker, 1996; Heschel, 2010). God sent Moses to lead Israel. Therefore, when leaders attempted to challenge Moses's authority, they received harsh punishments for their rebellion. When Israelite leaders Korah, Dathan, and Abiram challenged the legitimacy of Moses's leadership over Israel, Moses responded with the perspective that his legitimacy, indeed his very calling, came from God:

> Hereby you shall know that the Lord has sent me to do all these works, and that it has not been of my accord. If these men die as all men die, or if they are visited by the fate of all mankind, then the Lord has not sent me. But if the Lord creates something new, and the ground opens its mouth and swallows them up with all that belongs to them, and they go down alive into Sheol [the grave], then you shall know that these men have despised the Lord. (Numbers 16:28–30)

After Moses's pronouncement, as the account in the book of Numbers explains, the ground opened up and swallowed up Moses's critics. They died because they dared to challenge God's prophet.

Granted, it is not likely that all African Americans had the fate of Moses's opponents in the Numbers account in mind when considering Obama's prophetic status. However, The Exodus, as a metaphoric source of political agency, has functioned as a discursive lens for African Americans to use in interpreting the material world (Feiler, 2009; Glaude Jr., 2012; Raboteau, 1994; Selby, 2008). Within the context of The Exodus, Obama's ethos and legitimacy as a divinely appointed prophet were secure. With prophetic status, there was no need to challenge him because he was the one with the task of challenging power structures. The dual nature of his identity as a prophet-politician insulated him against criticism for inaction on racial battlegrounds. Just like the children of Israel needed to be patient during the trek to the Promised Land, African Americans needed to be patient as their Moses led them to the Promised Land of freedom, justice, and equality.

Additionally, this discursive lens positioned critics such as Dyson, Smiley, and West as contemporary manifestations of Korah, Dathan, and Abiram. That is, they were cast as jealous leaders motivated by their own interests, not by the sacred values of the prophetic tradition (Chicago Defender, 2010; Coley, 2010). The dual nature of Obama's prophetic-political identity holds another important implication: it suggests that African Americans must reimagine prophetic modes of political engagement. If Obama is Moses, then they cannot criticize him. However, speaking truth to power has been the dominant form of African American political engagement since slavery. Within the framework of The Exodus, the people of Israel earned God's favor when they supported the prophets that he sent. Prophetic engagement, in the age of Obama, required that African Americans use their prophetic energies to support Obama, not to critique him. It was almost as if questioning the prophetic leader was blasphemy. This perspective manifested itself in the racial pass that many African Americans appeared to give Obama (Hutchinson, 2010; Stolberg, 2010). Simply put, Obama's Moses persona removed the foundation of African American political engagement. That is, the perception that Obama was Moses left African Americans without a voice in the public square—they had their divinely appointed leader, and they should trust him to do the work of upholding sacred values. Silence and obedience, not engagement, was what the age of Obama called for in the Black community. In this way, prophetic forms of political engagement were constrained within a framework in which challenging Obama was discouraged as inappropriate. Dyson attempted to address this constraint by challenging the very prophetic identity that seemed to stifle dissent and debate.

OBAMA AS PHARAOH

Dyson used The Exodus as a means of divorcing Obama from the prophetic persona that had been linked with his presidency. In response to the perspective that Obama was Moses, Dyson offered a counter narrative: "You think Obama is Moses. He is not Moses; he's Pharaoh" (as cited in Smiley, 2010). This harsh statement was met with a chorus of boos from the crowd. However, Dyson responded to the audience with the statement, "I'm just talking about his office" (as cited in Smiley, 2010). In calling Obama Pharaoh, Dyson was not trying to disparage or delegitimize the president as much as he was seeking to rearticulate a perspective of how African Americans should view him. In the ancient story, Pharaoh, as king of Egypt, sat on the seat of power. He was the target of Moses's prophetic pronouncements, supplications, and condemnations. Moses, as God's prophet, pressured Pharaoh to liberate Israel from slavery. Within the interpretive framework of The Exodus, Dyson's purpose was to argue that Obama's primary position was that of a politician. As a politician, he was not above criticism or accountability. In a sense, Dyson was seeking to locate rhetorical resources to keep alive the prophetic tradition in the age of Obama. As long as Obama was viewed through the lens of Moses, prophetic forms of political engagement were threatened. As Moses, Obama was protected from criticism. However, the metaphor "Obama is Pharaoh" placed responsibility on African Americans to hold him accountable to his use of power. Dyson's goal was to dissociate Obama from the prophetic legacy of Martin Luther King Jr.:

> Black people think that Obama is Martin Luther King Jr. Excuse me! Martin Luther King Jr. shed blood in Memphis. From that blood and the soil in which that blood was mixed sprouted every ability of Black people in a post-King era to survive. . . . So don't tell me you stencil his [Obama's] face next to King's and they're the same. (As cited in Smiley, 2010)

The age of Obama witnessed numerous attempts to link the prophetic and the political in the person of Obama (Gitell, 2008; Hawthorne, 2008; James, 2009; Smiley, 2013; West, 2011). At numerous points during his comments, Dyson was careful to contextualize his critique of the president against the backdrop of his love for him: "When you talk to Mr. Obama, I love him. I love him like my brother because I'm so proud of him" (as cited in Smiley, 2010). His affirmations of Obama suggest that his motivation was not to castigate the president but rather to resituate his importance within the Black political imagination—even to empower African Americans to provoke Obama to use his political office for prophetic ends. Dyson's use of The Exodus suggests that King and Obama operated from completely different political ideologies. King, as a prophet, operated from the standpoint that God's primary focus was on the oppressed. He sacrificed his life for sacred values that society had abandoned:

> I choose to identify with the underprivileged. I choose to identify with the poor. I choose to give my life for the hungry. I choose to give my life for those who have been left out of the sunlight of opportunity. I choose to live for and with those who find themselves seeing life as a long and desolate corridor with no exit sign. This is the way I'm going. If it means suffering a little bit, I'm going that way. If it means sacrificing, I'm going that way. If it means dying for them, I'm going that way, because I heard a voice saying, "Do something for others." (As cited in Garrow, 1986, p. 524)

Obama, as a politician, privileged expediency, compromise, and public approval as key factors in developing a policy agenda. His decisions were calculated and measured. King, as prophet, rejected the status quo as immoral. Obama, as politician, received his power from the status quo. While African Americans had every right to be excited and proud about Obama's historic election, Dyson warned them not to "mistake cultural pride for political accountability" (as cited in Smiley, 2010). Therefore, he used The Exodus to create a discursive space in which African Americans could still be excited about Obama's historic election while at the same time recognizing their responsibility to hold him accountable for his policies in the Black community. Accountability, from Dyson's standpoint, was crucial to pushing Obama in a direction consistent with the need of the Black community.

The importance of this accountability is that speaking truth to power had been the dominant mode of African American political agency throughout the nation's history. Now, in the age of Obama, this agency was threatened by the perspective that Obama, as Moses, was not to be criticized. The purpose of this association, then, had very little to do with communicating a message to the president and very much to do with preserving the prophetic roots of African American political agency that might be threatened by perspectives that linked Obama with Moses and Martin Luther King Jr. By decentering or reducing Obama's prophetic identity, Dyson sought to restore Black political agency. As he argued, "Black leadership is about

Figure 4.3 Contrary to popular opinion, Dyson argued that Barack Obama was not the heir to Martin Luther King Jr.'s prophetic legacy. (From Smiley, 2010. © 2010 by C-SPAN.)

reinterpreting the fundamental premises of American democracy so that the ideals after which they aim can be embodied and the noble goals that they articulate can be lived up to" (as cited in Smiley, 2010; see Figure 4.3). From this standpoint, Dyson sought to generate a greater sense of Black responsibility in terms of the exercise of political agency when it comes to Obama by superseding the metaphor "Obama is Moses" with the metaphor "African Americans are Israel."

AFRICAN AMERICANS AS ISRAEL

Identifying Obama as Pharaoh empowered African Americans with responsibility to confront him on persistent injustices in society, contemporary Egypt:

> It is time to say to Pharaoh . . . let our resources go. Let that money go. Let that love flow. I know White folk don't want you to love us, but you came from us. Before they knew you, we loved you. We birthed you. We gave you acceptance. You were biracial, but Black folk made you a Black man in America. (As cited in Smiley, 2010)

In situating his comments within the interpretive framework of The Exodus, Dyson repositioned Obama as the rightful recipient of criticism. The goal of situating Obama as Pharaoh was not to segregate him from African Americans but to locate a point of identification with his historic presidency in a way that did not rob African American leaders of their political agency.

The notion of a Black agenda was controversial because of the perception that it privileged one group of people over others. However, leaders such as Dyson were operating from a prophetic tradition that is fundamentally concerned with the oppressed members of society (Cone, 1997; Darsey, 1999; Heschel, 2010). The Exodus and prophetic tradition teach that society is only as strong as its weakest members. Therefore, this configuration allowed Dyson and others to situate their calls for a Black agenda as an attempt to "express ... ultimate patriotism" (as cited in Smiley, 2010). That is, the interpretive framework of The Exodus fostered an understanding that America would only grow strong if the nation took action to strengthen its weakest citizens, eradicating structures of oppression. This belief was at the heart of calls for a Black agenda. Therefore, when reports began to surface that African Americans and Hispanics continued to suffer under the intense weight of economic recession, leaders such as Dyson were quick to call for additional reforms and policies to address the specific issues that those communities were facing. Within the framework that Dyson provided in The Exodus, African Americans were not wrong to hold Obama accountable. As Dyson argued, they were only treating him in a manner consistent with every other president:

> I tell you Mr. Obama, to deal with the Black agenda is what every president before you had to do. How you going to be any different? Abraham Lincoln had to deal with race. George Washington had to deal with race. LBJ had to deal with race. How come you the first president that ain't got to deal with race? ... If you want to be great, deal with the Negro question. (As cited in Smiley, 2010)

Dyson argued that those who reject the notion that the president needed a Black agenda failed to see that the basis of democratic engagement was to be found in different groups pressuring the president to act on issues facing specific groups through policy: "Latinos asking him for something; they got it.

Gay and Lesbians asked him, 'deal with Don't Ask, Don't Tell'; dealt with it. . . . All of those are specific entities . . . why is it when it comes to Black folk, we are persona non grata?" Therefore, Dyson grounded African American identity within the context of The Exodus, situating Obama as Pharaoh and African Americans as Israel to situate the people with the political agency needed to advocate for policies devoted to improving their condition in the nation.

CONCLUSION

From the standpoint of his critics, Obama's election has been a blessing and a curse. It has been a blessing in that his historic election (and reelection) has served as a source of great pride in the Black community. However, it has also been a curse in that it has constrained Black political agency due to Obama's identity as a deliverer in the tradition of Moses and King. In this chapter, I drew on the C-SPAN Video Library to explore how Dyson used The Exodus metaphorically at Tavis Smiley's forum to dissociate Obama from the legacy of Martin Luther King Jr. and the prophetic tradition. Dyson's use of The Exodus to discuss Obama's relationship and responsibility to the Black community highlights the fact that the biblical narrative continues to influence the political and cultural imagination of the Black community. Dyson's rearticulation of Obama's identity as Pharaoh demonstrates how metaphoric shifts function in rhetoric to alter perspectives and to advance agendas within various sociopolitical contexts. By identifying Obama as Pharaoh, Dyson created a discursive space for African Americans to exercise the prophetic forms of political engagement that characterized the civil rights movement. He also removed Obama's status as divinely legitimized by characterizing him as Pharaoh. His use of The Exodus demonstrates the importance of dominant cultural metaphors in articulating, negotiating, and debating various views and perspectives in the public square.

From Dyson's standpoint, Obama's status as a deliverer in The Exodus/prophetic tradition is of great danger to the Black community. In the original Exodus story, Moses had the opportunity to choose between political leadership as king of Egypt and prophetic leadership as God's prophet to Israel. His decision to choose the prophetic over the political is hailed throughout the Scriptures as to be a prophetic leader over a political leader:

> By faith Moses, when he was grown up, refused to be called the son of Pharaoh's daughter, choosing rather to be mistreated with the people of God than to enjoy the fleeting pleasures of sin. He considered the reproach of Christ greater wealth than the treasures of Egypt, for he was looking to the reward. (Hebrews 11:24–26)

His decision to side with Israel was hailed as the right decision because God was on the side of the oppressed.

This anecdote from the biblical Exodus highlights the danger that leaders such as Smiley, West, and Dyson perceived in Obama's identity as a prophetic deliverer. Obama had chosen political leadership instead of prophetic leadership. To hail him as a prophetic deliverer while he occupied political spaces restricted the Black community from holding him accountable to the exercise of political power. At the heart of these critiques, then, is the establishment of the fact that Obama operates from a fundamentally different perspective than did Moses and King. From the perspective of Dyson, understanding this reality would equip African Americans with the conceptual resources to hold Obama accountable to his exercise of power.

This brief analysis is part of a broader book project that I have undertaken. This project explores the role of Martin Luther King Jr.'s legacy in the age of Obama. In this undertaking, I find myself greatly indebted to the C-SPAN Video Library. The access that the Archives provides to events and forums such as Tavis Smiley's *State of the Black Union* series and isolated events like the one I focused on in this chapter make my research possible. As I continue to finish this project, the Archives will continue to serve as the hidden gem of my book research.

CHAPTER 5

GOING BEYOND THE HEADLINES: THE C-SPAN ARCHIVES, *GRASSROOTS '84*, AND NEW DIRECTIONS IN AMERICAN POLITICAL HISTORY

Kathryn Cramer Brownell, Purdue University

"U.S.A.! U.S.A.!" These chants followed President Ronald Reagan as he stumped on the campaign trail across the country. The Great Communicator was also the Great Campaigner, and the 1984 election showed how Ronald Reagan's team could package effectively an electoral message that sold nationalism and the proud declaration that "it is morning again in America." The Republican campaign used a recent song by Lee Greenwood to unify communities across the country behind the lyrics that asserted, "I'm proud to be an American, where at least I know I'm free. And I won't forget the men who died who gave that flag to me—and I'll gladly stand up, next to you, and defend her still today. Cuz there ain't no doubt I love this land. God bless the USA" (Jamieson, 1996, p. 449). The 1984 Olympics contributed to a celebratory, patriotic atmosphere. The Soviet Union's boycott eased the way for American athletic victories, and the shift toward a privatization model provided a dual cause of celebrating both American athletes on the field and the savviness of American businesses in the marketplace (Troy, 2005). Ronald Reagan had promised a better future for Americans four years earlier with a pledge to downsize government social programs, advance free market principles, and stand tall again in foreign policy. The 1984 election and his sweeping electoral victory—a decisive win of 525 electoral votes to 12 in favor of the former actor—showed how far the country had come with regard to embracing the ideas of the Reagan revolution and the president's powerful promotion of nationalism. Or did it?

Scholars have pointed to the 1984 campaign as the triumph of Reagan's rhetoric despite the persistence of the less-than-celebratory reality for the majority of Americans. The president's "Morning in America" campaign sold a rosy picture of life under the Reagan administration that overlooked the bitter debates over budget cuts and the slow progress of an economic recovery that seemed to benefit the wealthy, not the middle class Americans featured in Republican political advertising (Jacobs & Zelizer, 2011). As Kathleen Hall Jamieson (1996) notes in her study of the campaign, Reagan's overwhelming victory pointed to the political capital generated by the promotion of "peace, prosperity, patriotism, and presidential preemption" (p. 458). With Reagan winning the largest landslide victory since Franklin D. Roosevelt's 1936 defeat of Alf Landon, scholars have studied the policies, rhetoric, and effective messaging campaign that allowed Ronald Reagan to convince working- and middle-class Americans that they were better off than they were four years ago. In this capacity, the 1984 election reflects broader historical interpretations of the 1980s as a decade shaped by Ronald Reagan's presidency and the economic and political triumph of the New Right (Phillips-Fein, 2009; Troy, 2005; Wilentz, 2008). The first wave of historical scholarship on the 1980s overwhelmingly has produced an analysis of the period by focusing on the popular president and debating the validity and the meaning of the notion of a "Reagan Revolution."[1] But as Martin (2011) has recently observed, the emphasis on Reagan overlooks the debates about liberalism, civil rights, feminism, and foreign policy that permeated both popular culture and local politics and that formed an oppositional alternative to the celebration and growth of conservatism in the 1980s.

The C-SPAN network provides a window into local communities to illuminate the varied ways in which individuals engaged with national politics during the 1984 election. Programming covered candidate speeches, both on the primary trail and during the national election, as well as debates and accounts of smaller communities across the country. The C-SPAN Archives, which holds all of these programs, thus offers sources that can complicate, challenge, and expand our understanding of presidential elections and the 1980s more broadly. Furthermore, the material in the Archives, which has not yet been used by historians, offers avenues and ideas for how scholars can study recent American history. David Greenberg (2012), a scholar whose work transcends the political history and media studies divide, wrote a recent essay assessing the problematic neglect of television sources by historians. Sure, Greenberg argues, political historians acknowledge the importance of media and public opinion in American politics and they reference the central role of media spectacle in political mobilizations such as the civil rights movement or the New Left and anti–Vietnam War campaigns. But, while most prominent political historians reference the power of television in post-WWII American society, a glance at their footnotes shows that few actually watch broadcasts of major political events and analyze the nuances of these broadcasts. Greenberg (2012) contends that this is a major blind spot for historians. In part, this neglect of television comes from a proclivity among political historians to prioritize written sources and archival material and a tendency to see television as a "cursory part" of American life (p. 189). In this, historians could benefit by incorporating sources and methodological frameworks from scholars in the communication fields who have moved away from ideas of "technological determinism" and have examined the ways in which the political process, cultural values, economic pressures, and social structures shape and are shaped by technological development (Douglas, 2012).

Especially for historians studying the controversial terrain of recent American history, an analysis of television coverage of events is essential as, increasingly, written primary sources do not capture the nuances of the American experience (Greenberg, 2012). Over the past 30 years, television has served as a common reference point for Americans across regions and space; thus historians have the challenge of examining television sources more thoroughly to understand what exactly this reference point is, how it has been constructed, and the subsequent ramifications. In this capacity, the C-SPAN Archives holds a wealth of information to help scholars understand American political and media development and ways in which citizens have responded to, engaged with, and perceived these national developments.

Programming during and coverage of the 1984 election, especially the *Grassroots '84* series, provide useful case studies for how C-SPAN programs can help historians examine the political past in ways that go beyond a mere assessment of the major headlines of the day, beyond the slogan "Morning in America," and beyond conclusions drawn by a simple analysis of red/blue divides in the electoral college. C-SPAN programs documenting the 1984 elections reveal the persistence of a bipartisan liberalism in an era of conservatism, the shifting meaning of the "politics of localism" during the cable news age, and an electorate eager to engage beyond the public relations spin of mainstream news coverage, which increasingly focused on sound bites, slogans, and public opinion polls.[2]

THE C-SPAN EXPERIMENT: MEDIA COVERAGE FOR THE PEOPLE

A native of Lafayette, Indiana, and graduate of Purdue University, Brian Lamb envisioned a news outlet that would provide diverse, comprehensive, and direct coverage of the political process to enhance political communication between public officials and American voters (Frantzich & Sullivan, 1996). As far back as 1977, frustrated by the dominance of news coverage by the "Big Three" broadcast networks, whose programs highlighted the dramatic and the polarizing voices in movements across the ideological spectrum, Lamb proposed a cable network that would inform and educate citizens about the political process and issues at stake by presenting a range of perspectives to allow viewers themselves to decide on issues and candidates' qualifications. With the financial support of leaders within the cable industry, especially Bob Rosencrans and Ken Gunter, Lamb hired a small staff and prepared to launch a new cable network dedicated to televising public affairs without interruption, interference, or ideological bias. The Cable Satellite Public Affairs Network (C-SPAN) launched by televising the operations of the House of Representatives on March 19, 1979, the day that House-controlled television cameras first transmitted video. Over the next year, as the new network struggled to navigate the challenges of early cable television, it expanded its programming to include student seminars, chronicle "A Day in the Life" of representatives, and broadcast congressional and federal agency hearings.

As the presidential election heated up between President Jimmy Carter and Republican challenger Ronald Reagan in 1980, the C-SPAN staff worked to cover speeches by the two candidates at the National Press Club, to feature interviews with political experts, and to field phone calls from viewers about the election. With a tight budget, C-SPAN successfully covered a range of live political events and also fielded over 800 calls from more than 350 cities across the country to provide a discussion of the issues and candidates competing in the election. Several voices emerged in the aftermath of the 1980 election to praise the uninterrupted coverage of events that provided insights into the nuances of the national campaign rather than discussing the election as simply a "horse race" between the two presidential candidates (Frantzich & Sullivan, 1996, pp. 164–165).

Four years later, the network aimed to use the presidential election coverage to establish its credibility and emerge from obscurity. Just as potential contenders for the national presidential nomination had to take to the primary trail to assert their political potential, so too did C-SPAN use its coverage of the primary trail to show its political legitimacy in media coverage. The network covered the 1984 New Hampshire primary and Iowa caucus, and during the national campaign it took to the road to cover voter experiences.[3] One initiative in particular shows how C-SPAN programming can provide rich accounts of voters' interactions with, perceptions of, and critique of national politics. *Grassroots '84* had a goal of shifting coverage from "the candidates' points of view to examine the concerns of the people who go to the polls" (Frantzich & Sullivan, 1996, p. 172). Seven producers and a small production crew traveled in a Pace Arrow motor home to create a "video journey" that would show American voters' perspectives that went "beyond the headlines and political polls." During a time when television programming shaped a national identity, *Grassroots '84* emphasized "local color" as it featured the unique attributes of 14 cities and their residents across the country: Mission Viejo, Santa Ana, and Monterey in California; Seattle, Washington; Denver, Colorado; Tulsa, Oklahoma; New Orleans, Louisiana; Jacksonville, Florida;

Traverse City, Michigan; South Bend, Indiana; Harrisburg, Pennsylvania; New Haven, Connecticut; Westchester, New York; and Cleveland, Ohio (Lamb, 1984). The production team stayed in a local community for three days, interviewing its residents and civic leaders on a range of issues and concerns in municipal, state, and national politics.

The program contributed to the 4,000 hours of public affairs programming that chronicled the broader 1984 campaign, ultimately showcasing the effort of the network to provide a more detailed and comprehensive coverage of the political process (Frantzich & Sullivan, 1996, p. 174). While the election coverage provided the network with an opportunity to increase viewership, establish its legitimacy, and fulfill its new mission statement, the content of archival footage in the C-SPAN Archives also proves incredibly valuable for historians, political scientists, and communication scholars who want to study the intersections between local and national politics in a mass-mediated age.

The goal of election coverage to go "beyond the headlines" resulted in programming that prioritized a discussion of the issues and a critique of how newspapers presented the stakes of the election: the good, the bad, and the ugly. Each week a C-SPAN host would invite a journalist or pollster to the show, and together they discussed the headlines of the week. At the beginning of the program, the host invited viewers to "get out [their] morning newspapers, . . . take a look at that front page, and jump in and join us" (Jaroslovsky, 1984). The rules for viewers: have the paper in hand, focus in on what is in their local newspaper, and use that to have a conversation about national versus local events in a discussion aimed to "go beyond the headlines." Viewers called in to the program to share their views about the stories themselves and about how the media covered the issues and events differently in their communities. The call-in period frequently emerged as a time when viewers expressed their dissatisfaction with the "messaging" efforts by the Republican and Democratic campaigns or how newspaper editors framed national issues. For example, in a September 7 show, a *Wall Street Journal* correspondent, Rich Jaroslovsky, appeared to discuss media strategies by both presidential candidates. At the beginning of the program, Jaroslovsky discussed the Democratic presidential candidate, Walter Mondale's, "messaging problem" during the 1984 campaign. The C-SPAN host pointed to specific headlines in the *Wall Street Journal* and quotations used in the article about Mondale's messaging problem and asked Jaroslovsky to expand on the nuances of these articles.

This show covering the 1984 election reveals how C-SPAN programming attempted not only to inform and educate viewers about public affairs, but also to encourage viewer participation in a mass-mediated community through an analysis and engagement with various forms of media. During the same September 7 program, a viewer from San Antonio called in to discuss a story he had heard on National Public Radio over the previous week about the vice presidential nominee Geraldine Ferraro's stance on nuclear policies. He then asked for more details about a *Reuters* piece that discussed the competition and animosity between Mondale and the primary challenger, Gary Hart, and the debates that had emerged between these two Democrats about the future of their party. A viewer from Los Angeles called in to discuss headlines surrounding speeches given the previous day by Mondale and Reagan and the different ways the *Los Angeles Times* and the *Los Angeles Herald Examiner* had constructed the headlines and framed the story. She then offered her own views of the speeches while also asking the Jaroslovsky for more details about their broader context. During a program two days later, the C-SPAN host interviewed a prominent pollster, David Colton, who discussed poll results featured in *USA Today* (Colton, 1984). While Colton explained the "insider tactics" behind polling, he did so in a way that helped inform viewers about the industry and the broader issues at hand during the election. For example, Colton discussed how the deficit appeared in certain poll questions but not in others; this emerged as a simultaneous discussion of the place of the deficit in the election and the place of polling as well.

These programs repeatedly showed how these viewers did not passively accept the Reagan messaging and professional "spin efforts" but eagerly called in to the C-SPAN show to ascertain actively differences between myth, spin, and fact. Moreover, the viewer call-in programs more broadly provide an archival source that allows scholars to use new sources to evaluate reception and consider how viewers reacted to and understood political rhetoric. By the end of the 1980s, journalists and scholars critiqued the prominent place of the sound bites and the prevalence of iconic images in undermining democratic political discussion. As Todd Gitlin wrote in 1990, the previous decade saw the triumph of the "postmodern savviness of political coverage," wherein journalists and network anchors focused extensively on the behind the scenes construction of "spin" to give viewers an insider view of "politics." According to Gitlin (1990), during the 1980s, "the spectacular version of politics that television delivers inspires political withdrawal along the pseudo-sophistication" (p. 37). To show this, Gitlin examined shifts in network news coverage and radio talk shows and the statistics that pointed to a decline in voter turnout during presidential elections over the course of the decade that coincided with this change in programming.

But, C-SPAN's 1984 political coverage, especially the innovative *Grassroots '84* program, provides an alternative picture of how 24-hour news coverage could encourage voter participation, showing that engagement via the mass media and discussion of "political coverage" did not necessarily preclude a substantive discussion and promote voter withdrawal. *Grassroots '84* did analyze the ways in which news media framed issues and the behind the scenes strategies of pollsters and consultants, but it did so in a way that informed viewers and callers about both the stances and the identities of the candidates. For example, amidst an analysis of Reagan's messaging, a discussion emerged about which policies allowed him to create a particular image. Callers continued to ask about substantive material that would help them better understand the nuances of a popular slogan or sound-bite. While they acknowledged their understanding of how headlines aimed to present an issue in a particular light, or in Gitlin's terms they showed their political savvy by asserting their insider knowledge, callers overwhelmingly showed either an in-depth understanding of the stakes of the election or a desire to learn more information to become an active participant rather than an uninformed spectator. Election coverage available in the C-SPAN Archives allows scholars not simply to critique the rise of a mass-mediated political environment and its implications for national democratic discussions, but also to understand both how new types of discourse and styles of engagement developed within these dramatic media changes in the 1980s and the ways in which individuals navigated and understood these transformations.

By taking to the road and traveling across the country, *Grassroots '84* also captured the ideological divides between and within the Democratic and Republican parties that manifested on a local level during the election.

Committed to highlighting both sides of the political spectrum, the series made sure to feature prominent Republicans and Democrats in each of the 14 communities. As a result, this project highlighted liberal and moderate voices that historical scholarship had overlooked because of the effectiveness of conservative mobilization in areas such as Southern California (Seymour & Torres, 1984). The former mayor of Irvine, California, Larry Agran, discussed the political volatility in Southern California and the work of grassroots Democratic organizations across the state. Along with serving as a stronghold for the modern conservative movement, this region fostered a new version of liberalism rooted in a market-based individualism, supported by people to whom "New Democrats" such as Bill Clinton would successfully appeal eight years later (Agran, 1984; Bergeson, 1984). Because of its commitment to presenting both sides, C-SPAN gave attention to Democratic clubs that were not nearly as organized as the New Right networks that have garnered the attention of political historians. Thus, the C-SPAN Archives can help expand new scholarship into the rebuilding of the Democratic Party and the restructuring of modern liberalism in the 1980s and 1990s.[4]

The C-SPAN Archives also sheds light into the plight of moderate Republicans within a national party dominated by conservatives during the 1980s. During one call-in program, a self-identified Republican viewer adamantly wanted to discuss the role of religion in politics, and he expressed his sincere fear about how "nutty conservatives" led by Reagan and under the "dangerous" influence of Jerry Falwell threatened the moderate tradition of the Republican Party (Jaroslovsky, 1984). *Grassroots '84* provided a public forum for voices overshadowed by national parties and their candidates' messaging as they sought to reach out to like-minded voters across the country and have their voices heard. The research implications loom large within this archive as it presents a way to analyze grassroots political organizations and individuals who complicate narratives created by Reagan's effective "Morning in America" slogan. Reagan's electoral success hinged on the presentation of a unified, strong, and buoyant Republican Party, but with an examination of the bipartisan critiques of dissatisfied individuals across the country through the C-SPAN Archives, scholars can also go beyond the red/blue electoral divide and examine the more complicated and nuanced political reality on the ground.

FUTURE DIRECTIONS: EXAMINING A MASS-MEDIATED POLITICS OF LOCALISM

The C-SPAN Archives can provide easily accessible sources to help political historians integrate local politics and grassroots voices into the study of national political institutions and events. As Brian Lamb discussed in the final wrap-up session of *Grassroots '84,* he hoped viewers had gotten a sense of the country and the communities through the series (Lamb, 1984). While frequently not "partisan" along national political and ideological cleavages, the series showed communities eager to engage with one another as citizens, local residents, and television viewers. One producer, Carl Rutan, discussed how the shows allowed many people who had never before had a chance to articulate their beliefs on television an avenue to do so. In a political environment in which media access had become essential to gaining authority, the program afforded opportunities for individuals to assert their perspectives. Rutan told the story of a Jacksonville school teacher nervous about appearing on the show, but determined to find the courage to do so because it allowed her to have her voice heard by sharing the stage with local and national politicians. Rutan considered how his greatest successes involved getting "spicy local people" on the air to bring these individuals into a conversation with not just local city councils but also Reagan and Mondale staffers across the state. As the program traveled to the fourteen towns across the country, it revealed time and time again that a mass-mediated politics does not necessarily translate into a passive, uninformed citizenry, but rather that it requires alternative forums for engagement and avenues for participation.

Studying the political history of the recent past demands a study of television programming and political performances. C-SPAN programming, both on Capitol Hill and on the campaign trial, shows how representatives in Congress and presidential candidates have responded to the presence of the camera, so speeches alone do not tell the complete story. The triumph and implications of "media-driven performative politics" in the wake of the 1960s must be understood with this analysis of the visual record.[5] The cameras in the House, and then in 1986 the Senate, allowed representatives to communicate directly to their constituents. This has made performance and provocative appeals a more central part of the process while breaking down the camaraderie and sense of negotiation between public servants. A new generation of media-savvy politicians, such as Newt Gingrich and the 1990

"Gang of 7," used the camera in the House to assert their national leadership and to reshape the Republican Party (Smith, 2011). But, C-SPAN programs, especially those such as *Grassroots '84,* show how a younger generation of television producers broke from the dominant trend in mainstream media, approached television as something other than "infotainment," and joined Brian Lamb to use the new network to afford the American people the opportunity to talk back to their elected officials and voice their local concerns.

Historians have analyzed the "politics of localism" that shaped grassroots mobilizations around issues such as housing policies, welfare programs, religion, gender, and civil rights in urban and suburban spaces across the country (Kruse, 2007; Lassiter, 2006; Sugrue, 2003). C-SPAN's *Grassroots '84* shows how the politics of localism in the 1980s adapted to changes in the media environment in the age of the sound bite. Despite the calls for "U.S.A.! U.S.A.!" that infused Reagan's election, a mass-mediated politics of localism persisted and flourished in contrast to this resurgence of nationalism. Rather than simply looking at declining election turnout, network television obsession of debunking spin and advertising in elections, and the rise of the "hipster insider," the C-SPAN Archives offers an opportunity to examine local mobilization and engagement with issues such as the environment, nuclear freeze policies, education, and business initiatives. *Grassroots '84* revealed a political awareness and mobilization that transcended a simple red/blue national political divide as Americans wanted to reinterpret politics to shape their daily lives, and they used their interactions with the mass media to do this.

The field of American political history has experienced a recent scholarly revival through an embrace of new frameworks, sources, and methodologies that have sought to bridge disciplinary divides within the social sciences, humanities, and the field of history itself (Zelizer, 2012). By using the C-SPAN Archives, political historians can use sources from communications and political science to better understand the connections between local communities, national media, American elections, Congress, and the presidency more broadly. With its efforts to link local and national electoral experiences, *Grassroots '84* provides a window into how to pursue social and political history in the mass-mediated age. In the wrap-up roundtable for the program, Carl Rutan astutely argued that the people he met in New Haven, Connecticut, and Jacksonville, Florida, were not apathetic, apolitical, or disengaged. Rather, they were passionate about local politics. Grassroots issues from environmental concerns to education to tax questions drove civic participation. People would turn out to vote, argued Rutan, not because it was a presidential election year in which ideas of "U.S.A.! U.S.A.!" motivated participation, but rather because they wanted to have their say in shaping local power structures and to weigh in on debates over municipal issues. In this context national media attention on C-SPAN generated political capital at the local level, and all of the producers attested to the eagerness and excitement of viewers and program guests to advance their perspective on a national television program.

Scholars have tended to portray the political and cultural changes during the 1980s and the rise of cable television as part of the commodification of American politics, lamenting about how spin and the reliance on sound bites have taken over substantive, democratic discussion. But, C-SPAN provides an example of how cable television also encouraged civic activism and created new bonds between communities across the nation, not just with national political parties and candidates, but with one another. Thus, C-SPAN not only made history in its new approach toward covering politics, but its programs—from those that focused on the legislative process to those that chronicled the primary trail, provided coverage of national conventions and political debates, and included the perspectives of ordinary viewers—offer scholars an opportunity to study social relationships and political engagement in a mass-mediated environment. Historians have begun to understand how television changed political strategies, encouraging politicians to prioritize consultants, advertising, and media image above party negotiations and patronage (Brownell, 2014; Greenberg, 2004). Studying C-SPAN Archives will allow scholars to look not just at how politicians have responded to these technological changes but also at how television has affected citizenship, voter attitudes, and local communities as well.

NOTES

1. Wilentz (2008) examines the ways in which conservatism changed American political history through an analysis of Reagan's judicial appointment and the effectiveness of Reagan and New Right Republicans in learning how to "seize and keep

control of the terms of the public debate." Troy (2005) argues that Ronald Reagan reconciled cultural changes from the 1960s into new economic attitudes toward the marketplace in the 1980s, calling the 1980s a moment of the "Great Reconciliation." Phillips-Fein (2009) argues that the anti–New Deal business attitudes and shifts in ideas about political economy with the celebration of the marketplace emerged as a lasting legacy of the "Reagan Revolution." While she examines the role of free-market businessmen in dismantling liberalism and allowing for Reagan's conservative triumph, she argues that Reagan's leadership was instrumental in publicizing and promoting these ideas throughout the 1980s. While histories of conservatism from the New Deal to Ronald Reagan's election include an array of case studies about the role of individuals, business organizations, religious ideals, racial politics, and anti-feminist mobilizations in creating a mass conservative movement during the 1960s and 1970s, these narratives focus overwhelmingly on Ronald Reagan as an embodiment of the success of grassroots mobilization. Reagan continues to reign supreme in historical analyses of the 1980s. For an excellent overview of this literature, see a recent roundtable discussion in Phillips-Fein (2011).

2. Sugrue (2003) uses and analyzes the term of *politics of localism*, focusing on citizens' encounters with local government over housing, welfare, civil rights, and Great Society initiatives, especially in constructing urban renewal policies.

3. Video coverage of these events is available through the C-SPAN Archives. See for example: Summers (1984) (http://www.c-span.org/video/?72090-1/new-hampshire-primary-), Lamprey (1984) (http://www.c-span.org/video/?72096-1/new-hampshire-primary-), and Black (1984) (http://www.c-span.org/video/?98708-1/new-hampshire-primary-). These are just several of the programs that chronicled the primary campaign, discussed the candidates, and received calls from voters who would ask questions and discuss their experiences in New Hampshire with the primary process. The Iowa caucus was also televised; see for example Jasper County Democratic Party (1984) (http://www.c-span.org/video/?124894-1/iowa-rural-caucus). A variety of other programs interviewed people and political commentators on the caucus's candidates and process. Footage of the Democratic National Convention begins here with Democratic National Committee (1984) (http://www.c-span.org/video/?124426-1/democratic-national-convention-day-1). Footage of the Republican National Convention can be found beginning with Day 1 here: Republican National Committee (1984) (http://www.c-span.org/video/?124531-1/republican-national-convention-day-1).

4. Political historians have overwhelmingly focused on the roots of modern conservatism in the effective grassroots mobilization surrounding anticommunism, suburbanization, and evangelicalism in Southern California. See for example McGirr (2002) and Dochuk (2010). Only recently have political historians begun to examine the shape of modern liberalism in the 1980s and 1990s. Two studies stand out for new approaches to this question: Bell (2012) and Geismer (2014).

5. For a discussion of the roots of these "media-driven performative politics" in California and how this became a national political style, see Bell (2012) and Brownell (2014).

CHAPTER 6

DEFERENCE IN THE DISTRICT: AN ANALYSIS OF CONGRESSIONAL TOWN HALL MEETINGS FROM THE C-SPAN VIDEO LIBRARY[1]

Colene J. Lind, Kansas State University

Each year the U.S. Congress recesses in August, leaving political journalists to search elsewhere for a compelling story. But in 2009, Washington reporters had only to drive three hours north to Lebanon, Pennsylvania, to see Senator Arlen Specter (D-PA) shoved, shouted down, and threatened with God's eternal wrath by citizens angry about health care proposals (Rucker, 2009). Similar scenes played out during in-district meetings across the country that month. The crowds that swelled high school gymnasiums, fire halls, and church sanctuaries took almost everyone by surprise (Urbina, 2009), and the vitriol expressed at these meetings concerned many. Joe Klein (2009, p. 24), for example, wrote that the imbroglio revealed a "public malignancy" that "threatens the democratic fabric of our nation."

Undoubtedly, the health care town halls made good television. C-SPAN carried many of these meetings, but the network began airing and archiving such forums long before the high drama of the Affordable Care Act. In 1993, for instance, Senator Russ Feingold (D-WI) earnestly answered questions at one of his Wisconsin listening sessions; Trent Lott (R-MS; 1993) joked with high school students in Southaven, Mississippi; and a casual and confident Bill Bradley (D-NJ; 1993) spoke with constituents on the Jersey shore. As with most congressional town halls in the C-SPAN collection, these examples barely resemble the more recent health care forums: fewer than 50 people attend, no one yells or carries placards, and the tenor of the dialogue is civil if not friendly.

While town hall meetings seldom become spectacles, the genre does encompass the possibilities, failings, and contradictions of representative governance. The term *town hall* harkens the New England town meeting, the *sine qua non* of democracy according to American mythology. As political historian Frank Bryan (2003, p. x) wrote, the town hall meeting is thought to be "real democracy—where people make decisions that matter, on the spot, in face-to-face assemblies that have the force of law." Town hall meetings therefore convey a "vision of participatory democracy" (Ryfe, 2001, p. 182) but give citizens only an indirect voice in political decision making. Although these events are sometimes referred to as *listening sessions,* politicians in fact do most of the talking (Kay, 2012). For these reasons, pundits might worry over the incendiary health care town halls, but scholars would be equally justified in studying the acquiescence usually displayed at such gatherings.

Whether dramatic or mundane, hostile or reverential, congressional town halls have value. There, citizens come face-to-face with politics, politicians, and other citizens—an increasingly precious experience in the media age (Hart, 1999). In addition, elected leaders can establish their legitimacy before an engaged slice of the citizenry because of the close quarters within the town hall format (Shamir, 2013). As ceremonies of American political culture, congressional town halls also serve as venues in which the cultural mythos can be performed and reaffirmed (Rothenbuhler, 1998; Ryfe, 2001).

Thanks to the C-SPAN Video Library (http://www.c-span.org), scholars have access to audio and video of many of these events, usually in their entirety.

Aware of the unique opportunity provided by the C-SPAN Archives and the peculiarities of town hall meetings, I analyzed 55 in-district public forums held by U.S. senators and representatives between 1993 and 2012.[2] My sample included meetings held in 28 different states around the country. Republicans and Democrats sponsored these gatherings in equal number. Collectively, they bear an uncertain resemblance to the direct democracy from which they took their name, but they live up to their reputations as sites of ritualistic interaction between leaders and citizens.

I found that in town hall meetings, legislators use a language of deference to establish and reinforce social cohesion between themselves and their constituents. Despite the conventional wisdom that politicians will simply say anything to stay in their constituents' good graces, deferential rhetoric is a serious and complicated business. Drawing on the cultural rules of polite interaction, as well as the unique truths of American culture, political leaders achieve the proper demeanor when interfacing with citizens only through rhetorical finesse, balancing the words of esteem for others with those of personal integrity and independence. The most adroit and disciplined politicians use this delicate linguistic balance to evoke relations of mutual respect between themselves and citizens. In their weaker moments, legislative leaders accept the risks of a more radical version of the language, honoring citizens by dishonoring themselves.

DEMOCRATIC DEFERENCE, AMERICAN STYLE

Deference permeates human society, as social actors of high and low status ritualistically honor one another through displays of appreciation (Goffman, 1956, 1959). Conversationalists use deference to mitigate face threats (Brown & Levinson, 1987). Team members rely on one another's specialized capabilities when solving problems (Houser & Lovaglia, 2002). Low-knowledge citizens defer to scientific experts when forming their opinions on controversial issues (Brossard & Nisbet, 2007). Deference surrounds us, and social science and humanistic inquiry have frequently mined it for insights.

Conventional wisdom, on the other hand, presumes that *political* deference is a straightforward matter. As the following critics imply, politics and acquiescence supposedly go hand-in-hand:

> Those are my principles. If you don't like them, I have others.
> —Groucho Marx

> If a politician found he had cannibals among his constituents, he would promise them missionaries for dinner.
> —H. L. Menken

> Politics is supposed to be the second oldest profession. I have come to realize that it bears a very close resemblance to the first.
> —Ronald Reagan

But contrary to the common presumption, deferential political leadership requires a great deal of nuance. Because of its cultural history and unique political system, U.S. politics demands an artful balance between respect offered and respect retained.

The roots of American deference go back to the 19th century, when the citizens of the new society developed a preferred style of social discourse in keeping with their egalitarian sensibilities (Cmiel, 1990; Smith, 1999). Particularly in the United States, says Goffman (1956, p. 482), "differences in rank are seen as so great a threat to the equilibrium of the system that the ceremonial aspect of behavior functions not as a way of iconically expressing these differences but as a way of carefully counterbalancing them." Consequently, Americans hold to "conventions of flexibility and conviviality," writes Barbara Kellerman (1984, p. 30), conventions that mandate that "a successful interpersonal actor in this country is to undertake frequent pro-social or friendly communications, and it is to avoid unwarranted expressions of dominance. Quite simply, we are of a temper that is both democratic and friendly" (Kellerman, 1984, p. 30). U.S. leaders must therefore symbolically defer to citizens because social cohesion necessitates it and American culture expects it. For a politician to do any less would seem antisocial or even imperial by U.S. standards.

But at the same time, leadership requires something more than pure deference. As Jennifer Lees-Marshment (2012, p. 165) observes, not just in the United States, but "globally, in established democracies, there is a trend towards a public that wants to feel a sense of involvement in political decision-making but [that] also desires strong, principled leadership." John Gastil (1994) argues that democratic leadership is conceptually distinct from authority, but lay audiences seem to conflate the two (Barker & Carman, 2012). As Tulis (1987) observed of the U.S. presidency, it was "intended to be representative of the people, but not merely responsive to popular will." Rather, "the president was to be free enough from the daily shifts in public opinion so that he could refine it" (p. 39). An editorial board in Alaska summed up the dilemma as faced by those serving in Congress: "Sen. Lisa Murkowski late last month again behaved in a way that has drawn both admiration and anger from her constituents—she reserved judgment and listened to all sides before casting her vote" ("Sound Judgment," 2013).

For these reasons, democratic leadership ultimately entails some deference—but not too much. As Barker and Carman (2012, p. 152) write, total defiance of public opinion "might not really count as leadership at all" because autocratic control makes social relations between leader and citizen unnecessary. According to Hanna Pitkin (1967), Edmund Burke argued that good governance demanded that representatives ignore the fickle and ill-informed public, instead relying only on their own superior judgments. While that may count as governance, says Pitkin (1967, p. 170), it cannot count as democratic representation. At the other extreme, absolute deferment is "a 'delegate' democracy where . . . there is little need . . . for formal leadership, since the views of the electorate should be translated directly into public policy" (Geer, 1996, p. 17). In both scenarios, officials renounce leadership, which by definition requires some level of affection between authorities and the electorate. And as most long-time associates know, maintaining affection requires substantial effort.

Several historical examples illustrate the point. Hebert Hoover, for instance, erred on the side of arrogance. According to Alan Brinkley (2010), Hoover's repeated missteps at the opening of the Great Depression communicated that he had no empathy for suffering citizens and was impervious to their concerns. Similarly, if U.S. politicians indicate that leadership is theirs alone to execute, they risk charges of egotism or even autocracy. Al Haig was a case in point, having never lived down his statement, "I am in control here," words uttered while President Reagan lay nearly mortally wounded at George Washington Hospital (Hohmann, 2010). Haig apparently thought the situation called for a decisive statement of power to calm the public, but his words had the opposite effect. Haig, the Army general, had not learned the cardinal rule of elected American leadership: never forget who is really in charge.

Conversely, politicians who seem too quick to appease citizens will be chided as weak willed and ineffectual. To wit, a leader such as Bill Clinton, even at the height of his popularity, made himself vulnerable to Republican claims that he governed by the polls—a sure sign of unprincipled leadership. Susan Milligan (2011) unwittingly testifies to the presumption that true leadership requires some measure of defiance when she opines: "Paul Ryan Ignores Polls, Shows Leadership in Budget Debate."

The most effective leadership demeanor lies somewhere between these extremes of indifference and concern, between independence and subservience. Effective leaders therefore must use rhetoric to negotiate the horns of this dilemma, conveying respect for others to the extent that they do not sacrifice their own credibility. Ironically, "elected officials must be both leaders and followers" in a representative democracy (Geer, 1996, p. 16). This is not a straightforward problem but it is a common one; political leaders face it each time they speak to the citizenry.

To further complicate such matters, town hall meetings represent a potentially uncomfortable encounter between people of unequal status. For better or worse, elected leaders generally occupy an elevated position above the average citizen, both economically and socially. But at the same time, an American sensibility indicates that *citizens* hold superior political power, at least in myth if not in fact (Mercieca, 2010). Likewise, the elected official has greater expertise and more sources of political information, but in a body ruled by a democratic majority, the opinions and experiences of citizens ultimately trump the politician's specialized knowledge. These paradoxes underlie all U.S. politics, but when leaders and citizens come face-to-face in a town hall meeting, *where the people themselves live,* the contradictions cannot be escaped. Under such convoluted conditions of power and differential status, how can leaders and citizens maintain productive associations?

THE LANGUAGE OF DEMOCRATIC DEFERENCE

Legislators respond to these dilemmas by performing the linguistic rituals of democratic deference, thereby demonstrating their willingness to abide by the unspoken rules of mutually respectful relations between U.S. leaders and citizens. As demonstrated in the meetings studied here, this delicate rhetorical dance is a two-step: first, sound appreciative; next, verbally accommodate citizens' opinions and capacity for influence. When strung together adroitly, these symbolic acts make "a concession to the authority of the sovereign people" (Kane & Patapan, 2010, p. 372) without sacrificing the leader's integrity.

APPRECIATION

To strike the proper deportment for leadership, legislators must first sound grateful. As Goffman (1956, p. 477) sees it, deference is "that component of activity which functions as a symbolic means by which appreciation is regularly conveyed to a recipient. . . . These marks of devotion represent ways in which an actor celebrates and confirms" relationships. Humans crave the comfort of the clan as well as individual freedom, so deference rituals must both present (draw near) and avoid (respect boundaries). Social life consequently involves a "constant dialectic between presentational rituals and avoidance rituals. A peculiar tension must be maintained, for these opposing requirements of conduct must somehow be held apart from one another and yet realized" (Goffman, 1956, p. 488).

To verbally demonstrate their appreciation, American legislators pepper their constituent meetings with simple and frequent expressions of gratitude. For example:

Figure 6.1 Rep. Elijah E. Cummings (D-MD) speaks at a town hall meeting held August 3, 2009, at the Maryland Center for Veterans Education and Training. Cummings and other legislators studied here lavish praise on citizens attending such public forums. (From Cummings, 2009. © 2009 by C-SPAN.)

Thank you for your comments. (Feingold, 1993)

I'm glad you raised it. (Lieberman [D-CT], 1999)

I want to thank Mr. Williams for your kind introduction and all of you for what you have done for our country. So often it is said that our veterans seem as if they are unseen and noticed, unappreciated, and un-applauded. Join me in giving yourselves a hand. (Cummings [D-MD], 2009; see Figure 6.1.)

When we do town hall meetings like this, I always start out with a couple of words of thanks. I say this from the bottom of my heart: thank you for the privilege of working for you. You are my boss. You and the people who live in the first congressional district. Thank you for coming out today. (Bonner [R-AL], 2010)

One might dismiss such statements as platitudinous, but they serve an important purpose. Anything but empty, these ritualistic expressions of appreciation testify to the speaker's desire to be in social communion with the listener.

Beyond the ubiquitous "thank you," legislators take special pains to sell the compliment. For example, Senator Lisa Murkowski (R-AK; 2009) opened an August 20, 2009, meeting by noting that "outside we have a beautiful Alaska summer day. And you all chose to be here, to give two hours of your evening, to offer your comments, your concerns, yours suggestions, your fears. And I thank you for doing this." Murkowski could have simply said, "thank you for being here tonight," but instead she built a case for why the citizens in her midst merited special recognition. Congressman Elijah Cummings, too, took time to explain what made his audience worthy of praise:

> My friends, allow me to begin this afternoon by thanking you for coming out. It makes me feel good. . . . Every time that I have come here . . . we always have a good audience. I want to thank all of you. We really have every seat filled. (Cummings, 2009)

In her ethnographic study of town meetings, Townsend (2009) found opening and closing dialogue to be highly formulaic, closely hewing to ritualistic expectations developed over time. The local meetings studied here also conveyed a liturgical, although informal, quality. Rather than following Robert's Rules, leader-citizen interaction is structured by cultural norms that require politicians to recognize the engaged people before them. Citizens express appreciation in return, thanking legislators for their presence, their leadership, and their work. One of Russ Feingold's (1993) constituents, for instance, explicitly told the new senator: "I appreciate your sensitivity to your constituents." Most participants probably do not consciously notice a leader's words of appreciation, but if these simple expressions of gratitude were missing, constituents would sense their absence.

Likewise, leaders lift up the people in their midst as civic minded and politically astute. As Rep. Dan Lungren (R-CA; 2006) told his constituents, "I appreciate the fact that so many of you have come out, and it seems to me that this is a great demonstration of democracy in action." Senator Ron Wyden (D-OR; 2010) said that "the gentleman raises another good point and that is, is it possible to take some sort of, I believe you used the word incremental approach."

Figure 6.2 Rep. Newt Gingrich (R-GA) addresses a town hall meeting on October 19, 1998. Gingrich indicated his respect for the audience by explicitly voicing his approval of their queries, thereby implying that constituents should question their leaders. (From Gingrich, 1998. © 1998 by C-SPAN.)

Before responding to an audience member, Tom Coburn (R-OK; 2011) expressed the same sentiment in three words: "two good questions."

As presented here, these statements may sound like so much flattery, but within the town hall setting they present the leader as almost devotional. Particularly when a questioner implicitly gains "a measure of control over the introduction of topics, and hence the 'agenda' for the occasion" (Drew & Heritage, 1992, p. 49), a deferential answer indicates respect for the space between questioner and questioned. For this reason, Newt Gingrich (R-GA; 1998; see Figure 6.2) tells one citizen that he asked "a very good, very sobering set of questions," and another that he raised "a very good point." In doing so, the Speaker of the House emphasizes the agency of the inquirer.

Too much appreciation, however, can be smothering, so leaders also use words to convey separation and autonomy. For example, when a citizen questioned Gingrich (1998) about an education-financing option being considered in the neighboring state, the representative said that he would "let Alabama decide for itself whether that's a road Alabama wants to go down." Texas Rep. Kevin Brady (R-TX; 2011) also sought to distance himself from one citizen, but for a different reason. When questioned by a constituent who disapproved of

Republican tax cuts, Brady responded: "With all due respect, I disagree with the way you characterized everything you said."

Nonetheless, leaders rarely choose words that explicitly distance themselves from citizens. More often, they find subtle ways to be present and avoidant at the same time. Lisa Murkowski (2009) illustrates this when she responds to a local physician speaking at a health care meeting: "I want to acknowledge you and thank you as a family practice doctor. You are almost a dying breed in our state." Murkowski's words draw attention to the citizen, presenting her as a person of special value in the community. At the same time, as a "dying breed," the doctor also stands apart, distinct from the people in the room, not to mention other Alaskans. With her words, Murkowski wove the doctor into the community but also left space for the doctor's individuality. Terms signaling presentation and avoidance collectively honor the inherent contradictions of democratic citizenship.

ACCOMMODATION

While Goffman saw appreciation in the everyday interactions among people, other social theorists have conceptualized symbolic deference as a kind of accommodation. These scholars foreground differences in status, expertise, or power, which create social divisions that might otherwise become adversarial. Symbolic deference naturalizes the resulting hierarchy, creating a buffer useful for smoothing interactions between people on different rungs of the social ladder. For example, Steve Clayman and colleagues (Clayman, Elliott, Heritage, & McDonald, 2006; Clayman & Heritage, 2002) argue that journalists display their *lack* of deference for the president through active, direct, assertive, and adversarial questioning. It thereby follows that a deferential style is one that accommodates others by making space for them. In local meetings, legislators do so in at least two ways.

First, the leaders studied here explicitly allowed for citizen initiative, symbolically opening the door to the audience's political assertions. For example, after an exchange with a constituent whom Bob Kerrey (D-NE; 1993) clearly knew, and with whom he disagreed, the senator invited his interlocutor to bring others into the conversation. He asked, "To get an open dialogue started, what do you think should be the alternatives" to lower mileage requirements on cars and trucks? His question sparked no broader dialogue, but the citizen did explain her position and, as a result, Kerrey was able to identify points on which they agreed, as well as reasons he supported lower mileage standards. Kerrey took a risk, granting a great deal of leeway to the citizen, but considering their differences, as well as his prior experiences with the constituent, it probably was a risk worth taking. In contrast, Kevin Brady (2011) used his more secure position with a like-minded person to open an exchange of ideas. When responding to a constituent's question about the growing *Federal Register,* Brady first explained his own bill to curtail rulemaking and then asked the audience member if "that is something [he] could support."

In both instances, the leaders spoke in ways that accommodated certain differences in opinion. Clearly, Brady had good reason to expect that his questioner would support his position, but nevertheless, in asking the question Brady tacitly acknowledged that citizens have their own ideas. Both Brady and Kerrey suggested a measure of equality between themselves and the citizens in their audiences. Differences in opinion may still divide, as they did in Kerrey's case. Even so, Kerrey found what commonality he could uncover, including a mutual desire to reduce oil imports, as well as a shared ability to opine on important public matters.

Second, leaders use words to acknowledge and accommodate citizen power. Rep. Barbara Lee (D-CA; 2007; see Figure 6.3), for example, told her constituents that their work against the Iraq War had resulted in specific legislative victories. Speaking of legislation to disestablish U.S. military bases in Iraq, she said, "That came from you, right here in the ninth congressional district. It's accepted now as a policy by both Democrats and Republicans in the House." She also assured her audience that a budget supplemental that denied more funding for the war—a bill many in the audience supported—was having its intended effect: "This bill that passed yesterday has them, the White House, on the defensive," she said. Overall, "the elections in November sent a strong message to the White House to do something," said Lee.

Two years later, on the other side of the aisle and within a different debate, several leaders assured their constituents that, thanks to the "huge turnout at meetings like these" (Grassley [R-IA], 2009), Congress would have to

Figure 6.3 Rep. Barbara Lee (D-CA) makes a point at her point March 24, 2007, town hall on the Iraq War. Throughout the meeting Lee reminded the audience that citizen activism had forced policy changes. In the context of other debates, too, legislators indicate that politicians ultimately yield to public preferences. (From Lee, 2007. © 2007 by C-SPAN.)

abandon comprehensive health care reform. Dan Lungren (2009) said that "the outpouring and passionate views of the public have made a huge difference in Washington D.C." Senator Grassley voiced the same sentiment, but he also reminded Iowans that votes matter most: "Every two years, you have an opportunity in an election; and there are significant times when elections have made a difference. Elections have consequences. We're finding that out right now." Lee, Lungren, and Grassley acknowledged citizens' political actions, implicitly encouraging them to continue their political engagement. More profoundly, such talk acknowledged and tacitly approved of citizen initiatives, crediting them with a relatively high level of political influence.

In comparison, legislative leaders speak circumspectly of their own power. Senator Joe Lieberman (1999), for example, was careful not to promise so-called "notch babies" higher Social Security benefits, despite what was then projected to be a $1 trillion budget surplus. Even with the extra public cash, Lieberman could only commit to his effort, not the benefit: "We're going to give it a shot this time—I don't want to raise your expectations or anything," he said. The distinction here is subtle but important: legislators may promise the moon when it comes to their personal efforts, but their political power is limited and ultimately overshadowed by that of citizens. "That's why we need you to keep pushing, keep fighting," said Barbara Mikulski (D-MD) (Mikulski & Sarbanes [D-MD], 1999) in reference to Social Security.

THE COSTS AND BENEFITS OF DEFERENCE

Duncan (1985, p. 262) observed that "superiors, inferiors, and equals use . . . ceremonies as social stages to display themselves before audiences whose approval sustains their position in the local hierarchy." By examining congressional town halls as a type of social ceremony, we find that senators and representatives maintain their positions, paradoxically, through words venerating others. That is, the legislators adhere to the American preference for other-directed leadership (Kellerman, 1984) and sustain the cultural mythos of a sovereign citizenry (Mercieca, 2010). Even so, it is entirely possible for leaders to rely too much on a good thing.

MUTUAL VERSUS ASYMMETRIC DEFERENCE

At its most egalitarian, the language of deference approaches citizens as political equals, presuming that they can form, hold, and voice their own opinions. The Bob Kerrey (1993) example cited earlier is representative of this stance. By asking a disagreeing citizen to share her views, the senator momentarily deferred to the citizen, accommodating her difference of opinion, and implied that others had the right to express their ideas as well. In that same exchange, Kerrey also asserted his own right to disagree.

At its extreme, the language of deference approaches citizens as political superiors, elevating their local knowledge and experiences above those of a distant or centralized leadership. Indiana Congressman Mike Pence (R-IN; 2010; see Figure 6.4), for example, joked that

> throughout my nine years we've done town halls on a regular basis, my wife says they're my anecdote to Potomac fever. She means things

Figure 6.4 Rep. Mike Pence (R-IN) speaks to constituents on January 7, 2010, in Bluffton, Indiana. In a self-deprecating style common among U.S. politicians, Pence joked about the "attitude adjustment" he receives when he returns from Washington. Citizens understand the irony, but repeated references to know-nothing politicians reinforce the conventional wisdom of American political culture that citizens, not leaders, know best. (From Pence, 2010. © 2010 by C-SPAN.)

that sound like a good idea in Washington before [I] come home, I go to a town hall meeting, and get an attitude adjustment.

Rep. Mike Lee (R-UT; 2011) of Utah was more serious when warning that onerous regulation is the consequence of allowing "laws to be made by people other than Congress. . . . The reason why we got rid of King George III is because we could not get him out of office." Pence deprecates himself with clichéd humor, while Lee gains Tea Party credibility by referencing the Revolution. Using slightly different styles, both Lee and Pence aligned themselves with praiseworthy citizens even as they distanced themselves from Washington and called into question the capacities and motives of other leaders.

In the meetings studied here, it was not unusual to hear both inflections of deference—and sometimes within the same meeting. Why the shape-shifting? Warren Bennis (2007) answers that effective principals will consider what is possible in a given time and place, offering a different form of leadership as needed to capitalize on a given situation. From a philosophical perspective, Kolers (2005, p. 156) concludes that sometimes political movements require a kind of deference that is critical and questioning, while at other moments appropriate action "is to be determined by someone else's judgment." Likewise, Fenno (1978) found that an elected representative's interpersonal demeanor is largely a function of what the leader understands to be unique about the district and the particular group being addressed. Barker and Carman (2012) argue that the cultural divide within the United States demands different styles of leadership, with red America preferring minimal deference and blue districts listening for more consideration. In the town halls I studied, I found further evidence that politicians must be attuned to facts on the ground when deploying a given leadership style.

Even if there are situational benefits to unbalanced deference, this analysis also demonstrates that it comes at a cost. Rep. Joe Barton (R-TX) paid that price when he briefly lost control to two citizens attending his August 19, 2010, meeting in Crowley, Texas. His constituents insisted that the congressman support militarization of the southern U.S. perimeter and shoot-to-kill orders for border jumpers. This was a position judged too extreme even for a member of the Tea Party caucus, but Barton had trouble finding words to say so, struggling through seven minutes of dialogue to come to a defensible position that satisfied his interrogators. He finally settled on an explicit statement of disagreement: "I believe in civilian control, and I do not want to militarize the border between the U.S. and Mexico" (Barton, 2010). This was a difficult turn for Barton because, up to that point in the proceedings, he had deferred to populist wisdom and reflected a deep suspicion of the current leadership in the nation's capital.[3]

Some 1,300 miles to the north at his town hall on health care, Bart Stupak (D-MI; 2010) adopted a style of deference moderated by a measure of self-respect. He opened the meeting by acknowledging the differences of opinion in the room, asking constituents to contact his office and expressing appreciation for those who came to ask him difficult questions. However, Stupak in no way denigrated his own leadership or that of the opposing political party. When the grilling started, the representative consequently held a relatively strong position. Stupak frequently corrected his constituents, explained his thinking in detail, defended his legislative actions, and insisted that participants show him and others respect by refraining from shouting, interrupting, or cursing. The hour-and-a-half meeting was tense and both sides of the debate were heard.

As these examples illustrate, leadership rhetoric is not unidirectional, nor is it inconsequential. Most basically, town hall meetings highlight the dialogic nature of public address, making them part of an ongoing public conversation. Interpersonal scholars have long recognized that the tenor of talk influences how conversational partners subsequently interact with one another (Bateson, 1979). Recent applications of social learning theory also demonstrate that, in a deliberative setting, communicators will model the civility or incivility of others (Han & Brazeal, 2013). This chapter indicates that the same may be true of oratory: citizens will respond to the rhetorical projection of leadership in predictable ways, choosing a tone that fits the interactional frame suggested by the leader's discourse.

In the end, even if situational exigencies sometimes demand a stoutly populist tone, asymmetrical deference cannot sustain itself. Demeaning fellow politicians is a reliable but lazy way to connect with American citizens who have been taught that politics is beneath them. Ultimately, however, a rhetoric that defers to citizens by denigrating political leadership sacrifices its ability to be transformational. American politicians instead must work hard to harmonize deference to the people with a language of inspired transcendence.

THE RESPONSIBILITIES OF LEADERSHIP

Ultimately, the language of deference speaks directly to the ongoing debate over political representation. After more than 200 years of experimenting, Americans are still troubled by leadership questions: Are elected officials to be trustees, making wise choices on behalf of citizens? Or should they be delegates, acting as a conduit for the majority's wishes (Barker & Carman, 2012; Pitkin, 1967)? Do legislators act in the best interests of their constituents when they embrace the most advantageous policy for their district or when working for the national common good (Disch, 2012)? As long as these debates remain unsettled, senators and representatives must answer to all at once. For this reason alone, members of Congress arguably have the hardest job in U.S.

politics, being forced to demonstrate allegiance to their party, to Congress, to the country, and to their home districts—all at the same time.

Meanwhile, scholars of politics and communication must wonder if the language of deference has kept up with the contemporary challenges of representative leadership. They might ask, for example, how symbolic deference works in a highly polarized, ideologically coherent political environment (Jacobson, 2013). The 2009 health care forums notwithstanding, informal observation of the C-SPAN sample studied here indicates that citizens who speak at public meetings largely share their legislator's partisanship and opinions. When listening specifically to openly hostile proceedings, does the language of deference sound different? Can the lexicon even be heard in such situations, or does it serve a different end?

Similarly, deference might be a useful construct for those interested in leadership debates. Others have found that congressional proceedings are mostly civil (Jamieson, 1997), which seems at odds with contemporary experience. Examining deference in floor speeches, committee meetings, and procedural discourse might shed new light on congressional operations in an era of elite polarization. Undoubtedly, the wealth of data in the C-SPAN Archives could be put to use researching these issues.

Finally, future studies might ask if and how legislative leaders indicate their devotion to citizens when those represented are *not* in the room: Can deference be heard as clearly in other kinds of political discourse? Since most people never meet politicians face-to-face, surely elected officials seek to meet the obligations of U.S. political culture in press conferences, blogs, and franked mail. Even so, the language of deference might sound very different when the discourse is carried via an official congressional Web page or social media, for example.

Until scholars provide more informed and formal answers, cultural critics will fill the void, assessing perceived dysfunction and its causes. Some say it is unfortunate that our leaders fail to "push us out of our comfort zone and make us great" (Friedman, 2011, para. 9). Others say that the problem lies not with our leaders but with ourselves, persons now unaccustomed to acknowledging "just authority" (Brooks, 2012, para. 6). In light of this analysis of deferential language, we might conclude that the real problem lies somewhere in the middle. In true democracy, that is, both the leaders and the led have their obligations, obligations demanding someone defer to someone else about something.

NOTES

1. Portions of this chapter previously appeared in Lind, C. J. (2013). Democratic deference in a Republican primary. In R. P. Hart (Ed.), *Communication and language analysis in the public sphere* (pp. 99–119). Hershey, PA: IGI Global.

2. Using the search functions of the C-SPAN online Video Library (http://www.c-span.org), I first identified as many meetings between 1993 and 2012 as possible, using search terms including "town hall," "listening session," "public forum," and "public meeting." I continued using different keywords until satisfied that I had discovered nearly all possible meetings. I next eliminated meetings that did not meet the following criteria: at least one elected legislator spoke at the meeting, which was held outside of Washington, DC, and some of the legislator's constituents were in the audience. Finally, to avoid oversampling discourse on a particular issue, I identified the main topic of each meeting and randomly eliminated all but 10 of the meetings primarily about health care. A complete list of meetings analyzed is available from the author.

3. See http://www.c-span.org/video/?295114-2/congressman-joe-barton-town-hall-meeting, running from 32:50 to 37:22 and 42:14 to 50:15.

PART III

RESEARCH CASE STUDIES USING SOCIAL SCIENTIFIC LENSES

CHAPTER **7**

USING THE C-SPAN ARCHIVES TO ENHANCE THE PRODUCTION AND DISSEMINATION OF NEWS

Stephanie E. Bor, University of Nevada, Reno

Advancements in digital recording technology have greatly expanded opportunities for broadcast news organizations to disseminate media content. It is not uncommon for television networks to use their websites as a platform to stream live video, as well as to provide access to previously aired content. In comparison to the space restrictions that limit the length of news stories on broadcast television, the endless availability of space provided by Internet technology enables news outlets to disseminate extended coverage of news by featuring special interviews and other video extras that are not broadcast in their traditional newscasts (Becker, 2008). While the amount of video made available on news organizations' websites varies, the C-SPAN network offers vast coverage of public affairs events through its operation of the C-SPAN Archives, which exists as a publicly accessible electronic database that allows audiences to view every C-SPAN program aired since 1987 for free.

It is significant to consider the implications of this distinct record of public affairs information, as the breadth of this database is unparalleled by any other news service. As discussed by Stelter (2010) in *The New York Times,* "no other cable network is likely to give away its precious archives on the Internet. ... But C-SPAN is one of a kind, a creation of the cable industry that records every congressional session, every White House press briefing and other acts of official Washington." In its diligent efforts to preserve and index video, C-SPAN presents the Archives as a valuable resource for historians, educators, researchers, and other curious audiences to search for information pertaining to specific people and public issues. For example, Browning (1992) discussed the importance of the Archives in recording the Persian Gulf War, explaining that access to congressional hearings, news conferences, and more than 300 hours of call-ins related to this historical occurrence continues to enable scholars and historians to generate a holistic understanding of the events leading to, during, and following the war.

It is also important to consider the value of this digital resource not only to scholars and historians but also to journalists and other media professionals. These groups can find the "unedited, long form, no commentary" video contained in the Archives useful for informing their own projects and investigative reports. Internally, C-SPAN employees can also use the Archives to perform more effectively and efficiently in their jobs. This chapter explores specific uses of the Archives by C-SPAN employees in an effort to understand the ways in which this resource can improve the quality of news media production and dissemination. More specifically, a survey of C-SPAN employees reveals that strategic use and presentation of video content that is extracted from the Archives can enhance broader knowledge of public affairs among both producers and consumers of news media. Understanding the ways in which C-SPAN employees use the Archives also has implications for scholars and historians, as the findings presented in this study highlight creative and effective uses of this resource. Before proceeding to an explanation of how the Archives can improve the production and dissemination of information, it is necessary to first describe the methods employed to generate findings.

RESEARCH DESIGN

A qualitative research design was used in this study in order to gain the greatest insight into C-SPAN employees' uses, objectives, and opinions related to the Archives. Specifically, the researcher used survey and interview methods in an effort to generate an in-depth understanding of individuals' experiences interacting with the Archives. Data were collected from a sample of participants that emerged from C-SPAN employees working in the programming, marketing, and administration departments and all managers. This represents a subset of the entire 276 C-SPAN employees. In comparison to other C-SPAN employees outside these departments, as well as broader populations of media professionals and audiences, this precise population was selected because of their frequent exposure to the Archives in their current positions. To elaborate, it was anticipated that these individuals' close proximity to the Archives may have allowed them to develop expertise in effectively using this resource. Data collection was completed during the fall of 2013, and all research with human subjects was approved by the primary investigator's university institution.

First, an online survey was distributed to all 276 employees in order to collect basic information about the use of the Archives, such as the frequency of employees' use and the qualities of their experiences. Questions on this survey assessed, for example, specific reasons for using the Archives and how participants utilized certain technical features of this resource, such as clipping and sharing video.

Second, in-depth interviews were conducted with eight individuals from the total population of C-SPAN employees whose responsibilities at C-SPAN required them to work frequently and intensively with the Archives. The communication director was helpful in establishing initial contacts with these individuals, and interviewees were helpful in suggesting others that could also offer valuable insight. A semi-structured interview guide was used that assessed participants' reasons for using the Archives in their current positions, and their understanding of this resource in relationship to content being produced and disseminated on other media formats such as broadcast television and social media sites. While the interviewer assessed employees' specific uses of the Archives, broader questions were also posed in an effort to understand how members of a more general population could improve their knowledge of public affairs using this resource. Open-ended questions allowed the researcher to collect unanticipated responses to questions and to probe further into novel information that emerged.

Survey and interview data were analyzed using a qualitative content analysis procedure. Following a close reading of written survey responses and interview transcriptions, descriptive categories were created to encompass an array of similar concepts and themes that explain how the Archives can be utilized to produce and disseminate news. This analytical reduction process revealed four major themes that characterize C-SPAN employees' uses of the Archives: (1) to improve media outreach, (2) to enhance the perceived accuracy of information, (3) to provide historical context for current events, and (4) to review and improve the quality of news production. The subsequent sections elaborate on each of these themes by providing a brief description of the theme followed by examples extracted from data analysis that illustrate its meaning and significance.

FINDINGS

Use of the Archives to Improve Media Outreach

C-SPAN employees explained that they used the Archives to improve their communication outreach with other journalists and media producers, as well as to communicate more effectively with their broadcast and social media audiences. More specifically, employees used the Archives to curate information for specific audiences by extracting short video clips from longer programs and sharing them via digital messaging platforms. For example, one interviewee explained that the Archives enriched her daily interactions with other reporters because they enabled her to supplement textual news articles with illustrative video. To elaborate, if she knew a specific reporter was covering a certain public affairs topic, she used the Archives to suggest certain video that the reporter could use in his or her story, thus subsequently furthering the promotion of C-SPAN programming. A different employee explained that obtaining specific video from the Archives allowed him to localize content for audiences in certain geographic locations to show how C-SPAN has provided covered news in a particular community.

Survey analysis also revealed that employees used video from the Archives to improve their media outreach on social media sites. This finding is supported by the design of the Archives' online interface, which features icons that provide visitors with an easy way to publish video on their personal social media accounts. For example, one respondent stated that he used the Archives "to share interesting snippets of C-SPAN programming on other social media websites." Many other respondents discussed the use of the Archives in relation to their activity on Twitter—a popular social media site for news—explaining that they published hyperlinks to certain clips on their Twitter accounts, "to direct their followers to specific content of interest to them." One interviewee emphasized the value of the Archives in producing visually appealing social media content stating, "We use pictures and screen grabs that we find in the Archives when we tweet out or post to Facebook." Employees also discussed their process of publishing content from the Archives on their social media Pinterest accounts in order to further promote a segment that was previously aired on one of C-SPAN's television programs, such as *The Washington Journal*. Respondents explained that posting video from the Archives on their social media sites functioned as an effective way to encourage their professional networks, friends, and family to watch C-SPAN.

To summarize, employees used the Archives to improve their communication outreach with other media professionals and audiences. Technical features of the Archives allowed them to send specific video that was relevant to specific audiences. Additionally, employees identified an important relationship between the Archives and social media sites, indicating that they integrated archived video into their social media publication as a way to broaden the reach of C-SPAN programming and to create a more dynamic way to engage audiences.

Use of the Archives to Enhance the Perceived Accuracy of News

Data analysis also revealed that employees drew on video contained in the Archives to verify the accuracy of news content being disseminated to the public. To elaborate, when writing news headlines to be published on

C-SPAN's website or social media accounts, employees explained that including a related video clip from the Archives strengthened the accuracy of their report. In addition to only reading about a particular congressional hearing or government event, C-SPAN audiences also want to watch the event unfold for themselves, and the Archives gives them the opportunity to view an accurate and objective depiction of the event at a time and place of their convenience.

In addition to using the Archives to strengthen the perceived accuracy of their own news organization, employees also discussed their use of the Archives to fact-check or confirm the validity of other media outlets' news coverage. Unlike C-SPAN, other broadcast news outlets typically report information through the lens of a journalist or political pundit, consequentially resulting in the dissemination of subjective and editorialized news. Interviewees in the present study explained that they drew on the unedited and uneditorialized recording of events contained in the Archives to validate the accuracy of other news outlets' potentially inaccurate or incomplete news coverage.

As demonstrated in this category of findings, C-SPAN's commitment to providing the public with an unbiased and unedited record of public affairs news is useful for strengthening the perceived accuracy of its own news content. Additionally, the Archives exists as a significant element in the broader news media industry as it functions to hold other journalists accountable for the accuracy of information contained in their news coverage.

Use of the Archives to Provide Historical Context for Current Events

The extensive amount of video contained in the Archives, which dates back to 1987, allows them to function as a valuable resource for providing historical context and increased understanding of events occurring in the present day. As discussed in survey responses and interviews, many of the people and topics that appear during C-SPAN's live broadcast coverage have a long resume of appearances on the network. Because all past television programming is both indexed and abstracted in the Archives, it is simple to use the database's electronic search feature to locate specific persons, hearings, or issues that appeared in past programming. For example, searching a specific law such as same-sex marriage generates a long list of videos of floor hearings, news conferences, call-ins, rallies, and other related events that highlight salient moments in the political evolution of this issue. One interviewee stated that he frequently searched the names of congressional representatives appearing in current coverage of the House "to research older event coverage that may be relevant to today's news stories." Further, he explained that juxtaposing historical and live coverage of a specific event allowed audiences to generate a better understanding of the ways in which current political affairs were impacting civic life.

Several interviewees also explained that the Archives could be used to provide historical commemoration when a public figure died. More specifically, the ability to access and rebroadcast historic video of a recently deceased individual is a popular technique used by employees to mark the significance of a death. For example, one interviewee explained his process of using the Archives to commemorate the death of former House Speaker Tom Foley (D-WA) on October 18, 2013, stating:

> We have over 500 appearances of Tom Foley in the video library so I've been tweeting out some of the great moments of Tom Foley appearing on C-SPAN. . . . It's the kind of video that no one else has because we're able to tweet out 25- and 30-year-old videos of Tom Foley in Washington.

As illustrated in this example, as opposed to simply announcing that someone is dead, the Archives provides C-SPAN with a more dynamic way to commemorate a public figure by historically contextualizing the significance of his or her impact on public affairs.

Analysis also revealed that the Archives could be used to stimulate controversy by showing audiences how politicians have reversed their positions on issues. For example, in February 2013 Florida Governor Rick Scott (R-FL) announced his support *for* expanding Florida's Medicaid program. On February 21, 2013, C-SPAN's senior political producer, Craig Caplan, tweeted a hyperlink from the Video Library (http://www.c-span.org) that depicted Scott rallying *against* government health care in late 2009. In this example, historical context for Scott's announcement functioned to stimulate media controversy as the Archives was used to show an elected official's inconsistency in his policy position.

The following quote extracted from survey data further illustrates employees' use of the Archives to historically contextualize new content:

> I have used [the Archives] mainly for historical research. For example, we made a poster highlighting our coverage of past conventions, so I researched dozens of clips from past conventions for which we created QR codes that poster recipients could use to view the video. I have also used it in research editing Booknotes/Q&A interviews, trying to fill in the gaps in transcripts and understand context.

For this interviewee, historical video contained in the Archives existed as a valuable resource for completing projects and other responsibilities in her current position at C-SPAN.

As demonstrated by this category, employees shared various ways that they used the Archives to provide historical context for current events. Analysis of survey and interview responses revealed that employees largely believed that their strategic use of the Archives to situate current events in their historical context improved the quality of C-SPAN's event coverage and, ultimately, C-SPAN's audiences' comprehension of governmental affairs.

Use of the Archives to Review and Improve the Quality of News

This final category that emerged in data analysis illustrates the ways in which C-SPAN employees use the Archives for the purposes of improving their own work and the overall quality of C-SPAN event coverage. In terms of personal improvement, employees explained that they interacted with the Archives to advance their knowledge concerning a particular issue or event, which ultimately enhanced the quality of their projects and the fulfillment of their other job responsibilities.

Employees also expressed the significance of using the Archives to review their work. One survey respondent said, "I use [the Archives] to critique my work and to save for my own posterity. [It's] not easy to get copies of the stuff you worked on." This quote emphasizes the uniqueness of the Archives in the realm of broadcast television, as it is rare for media professionals to have copies of all of their work automatically and permanently saved in a publicly accessible online database. In addition to supporting self-criticism, the Archives also serves a professional development purpose for employees who utilize it to increase the exposure of their work. To exemplify, one employee stated, "I have used the Video Library to see and promote material I have produced."

In addition to reviewing their own work, employees also discussed the use of the Archives to evaluate their colleagues' work. More specifically, respondents explained that the ability to easily access their peers' work enabled them to produce content that was both cohesive and consistent with other content being disseminated by the C-SPAN network.

According to the results contained in this category, the ability to review previously aired content contained in the Archives provided employees with the valuable opportunity to improve the quality of their own work and the overall quality of news being produced by their broadcast organization.

CONCLUSION

The purpose of this study was to explore C-SPAN employees' strategic uses of the Archives to understand the ways in which this digital resource can improve the quality and dissemination of news and knowledge of public affairs. Consistent with existing research concerning the use of the Internet by broadcast networks, analysis revealed that an important symbiotic relationship exists between C-SPAN's television programming and its online Archives, as employees largely envisioned the Archives as a resource for complementing and enhancing their broadcast content (Chan-Olmsted & Ha, 2003; Greer & Ferguson, 2011).

Analysis of survey and interview data collected from management and employees in C-SPAN's programming, marketing, and administrative departments revealed four significant uses of the Archives. First, employees used the Archives to improve their communications with other media outlets and audiences. By strategically extracting certain video clips and disseminating them to specific audiences, employees explained that the Archives function to increase the exposure of previously aired material and to promote upcoming television programming. Additionally, video from the Archives was frequently used to supplement text and other multimedia content published on the C-SPAN website and social media accounts. Previous research has suggested that broadcasters' use of the Internet as a supplemental medium that complements their offline products can enhance the development of their audience relationships (Chan-Olmsted & Ha, 2003). In regard to social media in particular, it is important to recognize C-SPAN employees' use of the Archives to enhance their social media efforts, as existing research shows that broadcasters that integrate social media into their promotion and branding communications strategies recognize the importance of this new technology to staying relevant in a changing media environment (Greer & Ferguson, 2011).

Second, strategic presentation of video from the Archives was used to enhance the perceived accuracy of C-SPAN's news content. To clarify, rather than just reporting an event using written text, employees encouraged audiences to visit the Archives to view the unedited video recording of the event for themselves. Further, it was discovered that the Archives could be used to hold other journalists and media professionals accountable for accurate reporting, as editorialized news coverage could easily be compared with the actual occurrence captured in the Archives. The ability for the Archives to enhance accuracy and accountability in the broader news industry is especially important in an era in which news audiences are increasingly more mistrusting of journalists. According to a study conducted by the Pew Research Center (2011), Americans' impressions of the national media have become increasingly more negative over time, and in 2011, 66% of Americans believed that news stories were inaccurate. The present study suggests that strategic use of the Archives to verify and fact-check news disseminated by C-SPAN and other news outlets may alleviate audiences' negative opinions about the journalism industry.

Third, the Archives were used to provide historical context for current events. A review of past literature reveals that the Archives have existed as a valuable resource for historians and scholars to enhance case studies of significant historical occurrences (Platt, 1992). It is suggested that new and creative uses of the Archives identified in the present study have implications for populations attempting to conduct historical research to inform current events. Finally, the fourth category of results in this study described the ways in which C-SPAN employees used the Archives for the purposes of personal improvement and to enhance the overall quality of news disseminated by their organization. It is concluded that gaining insight into C-SPAN employees' creative and strategic uses of the Archives helps other populations understand how they can best use the Archives in their own work.

CHAPTER 8

MEASURING EMOTION IN PUBLIC FIGURES USING THE C-SPAN ARCHIVES

Christopher Kowal, Purdue University

On March 17, 2010, C-SPAN launched the C-SPAN Video Library (http://www.c-span.org) in West Lafayette, Indiana. Prior to its initiation, video records were available for purchase and had been provided in videocassette or DVD format. The C-SPAN Video Library transformed user access by offering free, online, 24-hour access to video records of all recorded activity from 1987 to the present. C-SPAN's commitment to factual, politically neutral coverage, easy access, and clear presentation with minimal use of split screens and no overlays makes material conveniently available at any time and visually easy to review. Live coverage supplemented by archived video allows researchers to review material and supports linkage to facial recognition software for behavioral analysis, trend prediction, or use with other analytical tools used to study political behavior and activity.

The "Congressional Chronicle" provides a searchable index of all House and Senate floor proceedings, including testimony provided by administration officers and committee members. Recordings are linked to the *Congressional Record* as it is released. Programs are fully indexed to simplify review of congressional sessions and committee hearings, allowing the Video Library to be searched by topic, bill, speaker, member title, affiliation, committee, policy group, keyword, and location. Transcripts of individual presentations are offered with full text identical to that submitted by the individual congressional speaker. In total, this represents an unprecedented window into every aspect of American political function, including testimony and debate related to the legislative, judicial, and executive branches of government. Opportunities for cross-referencing and correlating information for use in political analysis, marketing, investment, and education are limited only by one's imagination. Policy development and rule change can be monitored by viewing the activity of House and Senate standing, special, and joint committees, which provides timely information to viewers seeking data effective in the formulation of proactive responses. Commercial media response to C-SPAN programming, in conjunction with metrics from online social and other media, have increased the impact of consumer and voter opinion on political and administrative policy while providing strategic information related to buying and voting preferences in return.

A recent survey by Hart Associates (as cited in Weprin, 2013) estimated that 47 million people watched C-SPAN at least once weekly. The Hart study noted that growth was continuing and highlighted the fact that the most significant increase in viewer numbers was attributable to increased participation by the network's largest demographic group, 18 to 49 year olds. In a press release on the same date, *C-SPAN at 34,* the network noted that Hart Research indicated that 89% of C-SPAN viewers voted in the 2012 presidential election, compared to a national average turnout of 57.5%. In addition, school and college faculty members are using programming and data for course formulation while students view C-SPAN in classroom presentations and use information from studies for research projects. While news viewership in the 25 to 54 demographic for 2012 was down at most networks, this group of C-SPAN viewers continued to grow. At a glance this would seem to support an increase in young viewers seeking direct access to unbiased records of political behavior for their own assessment through access to material presented on C-SPAN.

Political analysts, researchers, news commentators, and others are interested in developing their capacity to understand and predict political behaviors. This is vital for increasing their capacity for understanding events and their probable impact and for the formulation of effective response. The achievement of these tasks solely through an analysis of content is inevitably based on some supposition. An accurate understanding of content requires its examination within the emotional context of the situation or behavior from which it was initiated. Therefore, this chapter focuses on examining a recent development in emotion analysis and exploring how its use, in conjunction with Video Library footage, can improve the understanding of events and increase predictive capacity. The value of an accurate perception of the emotional tone and composition of recorded participants is incalculable. Research has shown that the perception of emotion by viewers is a highly determinative factor in viewer response (Buck, 1980; Russell & Fernández-Dols, 1997; Shields & MacDowell, 1987).

Until now, efforts to accurately determine the emotional tone of participant statements and determine likely viewer response have involved a significant degree of interpretation by the analyst. Each individual's values color his or her perceptions, making some impact on evaluation inevitable. Recent developments significantly improve reviewer capacity for assessment and prediction. The use of facial recognition technology (FRT) in conjunction with footage from the vast C-SPAN library of political figures and interactions offers nearly endless possibilities for researching the emotions and actions of political leaders and election participants. Using these assets, researchers and analysts can examine and contrast historical and contemporary behaviors objectively to extract a high level of understanding and predictive accuracy. The comparison and contrast of emotional behaviors presented by individuals in varied circumstances offers valuable insight into individual strengths, weaknesses, future response patterns, and capacity for effective leadership. Combining the results of FRT analysis with records of public response can provide a type of best practice approach to assessing the emotional behavior of political leaders.

TRANSPARENCY AND VERIFICATION

In recent years the assertions and denials of high-profile newsmakers and key political figures have been confirmed, supported, or disproved by the availability of C-SPAN's recorded video. A well-known example of this occurred on December 21, 2009. MSNBC's *The Rachel Maddow Show* presented C-SPAN video of a Senate proceeding documenting Senator John McCain's (R-AZ) October 10, 2002, objection, refusing a request for 30 seconds of time to Senator Mark Dayton (D-MN) during Dayton's comments opposing authorization for the Iraq war. McCain's comments in this video were a direct contradiction of his recent outraged statement that "never in his 20 years had he seen a Senate member denied just a little more time" after Senator Al Franken (D-MN) denied Senator Joe Lieberman (I-CT) a few extra moments during the debate on health reform legislation. Time for discussion was limited to allow the vote for the passage of President Obama's health care bill to take place before the holiday break. Following her presentation of the video, Maddow enthusiastically thanked C-SPAN for the confirmation video, saying: "I love C-SPAN. I love you guys. Never change. You are perfect in every way." Similar examples of situational changes in judgment have been documented in the actions and opinions of other political figures using C-SPAN video.

C-SPAN AND ADVANCED ANALYTICS

C-SPAN video has become popular with journalists and analysts who utilize its database for content, historical records of congressional proceedings, and other recorded material related to public affairs. The advent of new technology for emotional research, in conjunction with the comprehensive record of political action, offers an unprecedented and objective record documenting incidents of and responses to emotional behavior in politics. The research discussed in this chapter examines the impact of emotional power in political interaction, its persuasive and prejudicial effects, and ultimately the most effective use of emotion for building trust and confidence in leadership. This new technology improves both speed and accuracy in the analysis of political behavior, allowing examination and correlation with viewer and voter response.

In this chapter we will examine how the Noldus FaceReader software, utilized in conjunction with C-SPAN's archived material, can support a new level of analysis. This collaboration improves user access to data as a resource for new research on the impact of emotion in political behavior. Through the application of FRT, users are able to detect posturing and to differentiate between credible and mendacious commentary. The research shows that the predictive accuracy of viewer response is very high.

Beyond providing video documentation to establish facts, C-SPAN's Video Library is preserving a cultural record of political behavior and activity for historical review. The comprehensive coverage provided by recorded proceedings allows researchers to obtain information firsthand, whereas the reporting of a singular event, such as the passage or defeat of a specific bill, leaves questions that require guesswork or the investigation of additional sources to document a specific trend or conclusion. Researchers, analysts, and students alike can now study the actions and behaviors of government members, documenting facts and evaluating changing patterns in our social, political, and economic landscapes. The combination of live coverage and archived recordings of congressional proceedings allows viewers to examine and contrast contemporary and historical proceedings related to current issues and offers insights into the attitudes and historical behavior of representatives from each district, state, and political party.

Completely unaltered recordings allow viewers to make independent assessments of cooperation and conflict between representatives, committee members, and administrative or other individuals appearing to give testimony, effectively mapping the demographic and political topography of the country. Recordings of activity in committees from Agriculture to Ways and Means provide users the means to review activity in their area of interest, yielding analytical insights unavailable prior to C-SPAN broadcasts. Video recordings simplify the identification of key influencers, highlight group and individual presentations, and allow for user analysis of each speaker's perspectives, oratorical style, strategic approach, personal affect, effectiveness, and elicited responses.

Researchers are now evaluating the impact of emotion on message response, viewer perception of candidates' competence, and how these responses affect the promotion of voter trust during and after appearances and debates.

Myers and Tingley (2011) state that

> there is reason to expect emotion to have a significant impact on trust. Emotions have been shown to affect a variety of decision making processes and complex decisions[,] such as the decision required to trust political leaders with regional or national management. . . . [Such decisions] are particularly likely to be influenced by a person's emotional state. (p. 1)

With this understanding it is easy to see how political leaders need to understand the impact of emotionally charged messages on their ability to build trust and credibility with the public.

RESEARCH ON EMOTION IS IMPORTANT

The political implications of emotion are pervasive, having been empirically linked to perceptions of candidates and voter choice (Brader, 2011; Taber & Lodge, 2006). During the past two decades the study of emotion in social and political life has become increasingly important to investigation in political science, social science, and psychology (Ekman, 1999; Fischer, 2000; Russell & Fernández-Dols, 1997). The political arena offers an ideal environment for study because it involves national participation, topical importance, frequent controversy, high levels of affective response, and the availability of extensive material for analysis and through media participation and documentation.

Shields and MacDowell (1987) relate that "for the most part ours is a culture that considers emotion an immature, irrational and uncontrollable event" (p. 2). While their research shows that responses to emotion have historically been negative, they note that emotion may reflect positively on the speaker in specific situations, stating that emotion is most positively received in circumstances where its display is perceived as appropriate. Just as emotional behavior is judged acceptable and even desirable in sports and other contests, emotional responses in politics are viewed most positively when "some affective display is likely . . . and partisanship is salient" (p. 80). The authors are clear that individual responses are a matter of personal assessment in the context of the viewer's value system. A viewer's assessment of affective displays influences his or her perception of a candidate's character and capacity to handle issues if elected. Because candidate responses are seen as appropriate or inappropriate based on individual values, it is impossible to predict individual reaction. Shields and MacDowell (1987) further state that "it is a fact of political life that one's emotions can make or break a political image" (p. 78) and later suggest that, despite this fact, emotion appropriately presented by political candidates can actually increase perceptions of credibility and legitimacy. Both John Kennedy and Bill Clinton are cited by numerous sources as having benefited from this strategy, while Richard Nixon is the most commonly cited as an example of its failure. The authors of the study present their results as indicative of the fact that the political affiliation and gender of media representatives and individual viewers were primary determinants in their perception of and evaluation of candidate emotion as indicative of individual performance, making unbiased evaluation of political statements and actions as impossible as predictions of individual perception. Although most Americans view publicly displayed emotion as a loss of control and assign emotion a negative value in political activity, there are notable exceptions. Using the example of Proposition 13 and California voter outrage, Marcus (2000) points out the determinative factor when he tells us that when the expressed emotion (in this case anger) is not a feature of individual personality but rather is attached to an external situation or event, it may be a powerful means of provoking a reaction from the audience. In fact, these types of perceptions about political candidates have been researched, and evidence suggests that they have played a significant role in the audience reactions during past debates (Sears & Chaffee, 1979).

Research conducted by Simons and Leibowitz (1979) and Tannenbaum, Greenberg, and Silverman (1962) involving viewer evaluations of candidates after debates suggests that audience perception of a candidate's ability or inability to handle debate questions and objections is conveyed by the affective or emotional attributes of the candidate. These authors compared the impact of *need for cognition* and *trait-focused spin*. Trait-focused spin, something we might now refer to as *charisma*, was determined to exert the more significant influence by a wide margin.

Emotion has been used as an explanation for people's deviation from their normal behavior (Sears & Citrin, 1982). Contrary to this idea, emotion also has been proclaimed to be what causes people to hold dear to their values, beliefs, and attitudes (Sears, 1993). Regardless of which lens emotion is viewed through, an agreement has been reached that memory, evaluation, judgment, and action are also affected by emotion (Marcus, 2000). These studies offer a clear indication that emotion is perceived in highly individual ways. The researchers report that voters are sometimes affected with a need to hold to cherished beliefs, while in other cases they are moved to significantly changed behavior.

Anger has been shown to be productive of a more positive effect when portrayed as a reaction to an event and a more negative effect when seen as a loss of control. Until now we have lacked an effective indicator supportive of a reliable level of predictability of audience response to individual presentation on a given occasion. From Nixon's forced resignation under the threat of impeachment during Watergate to Clinton's survival of Whitewater and acquittal from impeachment following the Monica Lewinsky scandal, we are presented with the power of contrasting personal style and emotional presentation. Nixon's career was ended by scandal; Clinton left office with a 65% approval rating.

Emotion has long been an important topic of discussion in psychology (Ekman, 1999; Russell & Fernández-Dols, 1997). The appropriateness of emotions has been researched with regard to the outcome of political debates (Shields & MacDowell, 1987). Culturally in the United States, the expression of emotion or exhibition of emotional behavior is looked down upon as evidence that one is not always in control of oneself (Averill, 1980; Solomon, 1976). In contrast, Shields and MacDowell (1987) suggest that a show of emotion by a political candidate can actually increase perceptions of that candidate's credibility and legitimacy. These types of perceptions about political candidates have been researched, and evidence suggests that they have played a large role in audience reactions during past debates (Sears & Chaffee, 1979). However, the search for a clear understanding of human emotional response to political behavior remains a priority and the issue is unresolved.

FACIAL EXPRESSION AND EMOTION RESEARCH

Politics in the United States has become increasingly volatile and contentious over the last two decades. Since Newt Gingrich presented the "Republican Contract With America" during the 1994 congressional election, political polarization and antagonism in American politics has risen to historic levels. The growing friction between Republicans and Democrats and their constituencies has escalated steadily. In the process the American public has become sharply divided, and media news sources are now recognized by affiliation more often than by coverage quality. In this atmosphere every word and gesture of American presidents has been scrutinized, analyzed, and denigrated by partisans of one party, group, organization, or another. Perhaps for these reasons the importance placed on research studies of emotion as it relates to perception of political figures has steadily increased.

In an effort to diminish negative reactions, candidates have become more aware of their presentation style and are now training to improve their ability to use facial expressions, voice modulation, and body language to build voter trust and add credence to their message. While statistics vary from source to source, according to Mehrabian's (1967) formula, there is general agreement about the importance of emotional management and presentation style: 55% of a speaker's message is conveyed by visual cues, while only 7% is conveyed by the message itself.

Business executives and politicians across the country are engaging in training to learn to convey their messages more effectively. A variety of programs, including American Majority, Public Speaking International, New Strategies Group, Democracy for America, and numerous others, are training aspiring leaders in new ways of communicating. As candidates and their advisors work toward improving public image, researchers are pursuing a more specific analysis of the elements of emotional projection. Attracted by the possibility of understanding and controlling the elements that evoke voter approval, trust, and support, they search for a means of identifying fundamental elements related to appeal and indicative of positive voter response. The most promising asset emerging in this process is the development of FRT.

FACIAL FEEDBACK HYPOTHESIS

Facial recognition technology (FRT) has evolved over the last 50 years as numerous studies have analyzed the components of facial expressions and their relationship to felt and perceived emotion. Surprisingly, the discoveries made have involved the universal nature of the relationship between a specific facial configuration and the felt expression described by the subjects. While the social value of a given expression varies across cultures, the qualitative nature of the emotions related to feature and muscular configurations is identical (Ekman, 2003). So, while one's smile may be an indication of something different than that of an individual in another culture, the underlying experience of joy or disgust is identical and can be recognized by its musculature. This fact is the basis of our understanding of which muscle actions and expressions describe specific emotions (Wagner, 1997).

During his research for his book *Emotions Revealed: Recognizing Faces and Feelings to Improve Communication and Emotional Life,* Ekman (2003) made an interesting discovery. He found that he when he made certain expressions, he experienced the related emotions. This discovery supported his belief that the primary emotions he had identified were universal to all human beings. Earlier researchers, including Darwin, James, Buck, Aldeman, and Zajonc, have also noted a form of reciprocity between individuals, observing that a person's emotional experience or behavior can be affected by feedback through facial expressions from a sender or responder. Specifically, this indicates that not only do a speaker's expressions convey an emotional context but that they can invoke a related experience in the viewer.

FACIAL RECOGNITION TECHNOLOGY: EARLY RESEARCH

Woody Bledsoe, later accompanied by Helen Wolf and Charles Bisson, was a key figure in the earliest development of a computer programmed for automated facial recognition. Between 1964 and 1965, Bledsoe used a computer to recognize human faces in pictures. His system was crude by today's standards, utilizing a user-drawn map of 20 separate feature coordinates established by distances between features, such as pupil centers, and recording the information on a tablet that digitized the data. The system he created was used to search pictures of suspects to identify those with similar graphic features. Little information was available because Bledsoe and his associates were working with funding provided by an intelligence agency and disclosure was not possible. Bledsoe overcame basic obstacles, such as compensation for angularity caused by head tilt, and used measurements from seven heads to create a three-dimensional model of an average head in order to model positioning for the computer, creating programming to simulate heads in the pictures in a normalized front-facing position.

Bledsoe's work was continued at the Stanford Research Institute, where the speed and efficiency of the process was improved. By the late 1990s, several institutes were developing software programs for facial recognition (FR). The system developed by the University of Southern California in collaboration with the University of Bochum in Germany was chosen as the most efficient, and with funding from the U.S. Army Research Labs it was developed and sold as the ZN-Face software program. The program was installed at Deutsche Bank and was utilized by airports and in other public places. The system at this point had become sophisticated enough to make identifications despite hairstyle changes or the addition of beards, mustaches, and sunglasses.

Recent Developments

The next level of innovation was available by 2007 when a Minnesota company, Identix, produced FaceIt. Capable of identifying individuals in crowds from nearly any angle that allows some facial exposure, FaceIt can pick out someone's face in a crowd and compare it with faces from databases worldwide to recognize and put a name to a face. FaceIt has a competitor in Polar Rose, whose technology was recently purchased by Apple. This same technology may soon be available to consumers to open their profiles in various programs, thus replacing passwords. Now extremely effective in three-dimensional identification and hundreds of times more effective, even the advanced algorithms of these programs utilize the same essential principle of face mapping that was developed by Bledsoe.

Used in computer technology, information processing, and building security systems, and by identification and licensing agencies, banks, airports, homeland security operations, and law enforcement agencies, FRT has made an important contribution to the efficiency and security of workplaces and communities. Interestingly, the same technology that is used to link our social profiles with our cell phone pictures, and has replaced everything from fingerprints and passwords to lie detectors, has not yet been used in political analysis. But the potential for innovation and learning is nearly limitless, and it is likely that executives and politicians will soon be learning techniques specifically related to the elimination or inclusion of facial expressions in order to generate a predictably higher level of positive responses and develop an increased level of voter trust.

Understanding Emotional Valence

Noldus, in its creation of the FaceReader algorithm, loaded more than 10,000 manually annotated images into the program. Based on work that evolved from Ekman's (1970) *Universal Facial Expressions of Emotion*, these images described over 500 identification points of features and facial texture. The program utilizes the images and relates subject features to the models. As FaceReader scans a subject's face at a rate of 20 frames per second, it compares the individual's face to its catalog of emotional expressions. Attempts to create a false impression are normally picked up by fine differences in expression. For example, a posed smile has a different mouth shape and configuration than a genuine or spontaneous smile. Arousal and intensity are determined by the FaceReader program by comparing a subject image to its catalog of facial expressions, and differences are signified by facial tone and texture. In the scanning process the program measures seven dimensions of primary emotional status: happy, sad, angry, surprised, scared, disgusted, and neutral. The scan assigns values by recognizing the presence or absence of muscle configuration indicative of each emotion. A value is registered for the relative presence or absence of each characteristic, and the composite value is expressed as a positive or negative number indicating the emotional valence.

FACIAL RECOGNITION TECHNOLOGY TODAY

The process of mapping facial features in relation to emotional content is complex. But despite the complexity of the task and the sophistication of modern equipment, the premise remains essentially the same as it was when Woody Bledsoe first developed his program in the early 1960s. The algorithm is many times more sophisticated and, in addition to recognizing individuals, it can detect when a person is lying and can analyze personal emotion. Positional problems are resolved by a complete three-dimensional model built by the program that allows it to change angular perspective and identify the individual separately from the surrounding environment. Two algorithms are required to perform the functions of identification and affective state. An individual's affective state comprises three dimensions: valence, arousal, and motivational intensity. For the purpose of this chapter, I will offer a simplified explanation, noting that arousal and motivational intensity are reflected in facial tone. A simplistic but useful analogy might be that arousal is a response to noticing a need. Hunger, for example, is a state of arousal. Maintaining this analogy, motivational intensity would relate to how hungry a person became and what tension his or her need created, literally the strength of the need. Valence is a measure of relative attractiveness or averseness, commonly referred to as degree of positive or negative affect. Emotional valence is an expression of the relative degree of positive or negative affect.

THE NOLDUS FACEREADER

The Noldus FaceReader is likely to be used by candidates to help them learn to project a balanced emotional valence. Researchers now believe that the value placed on perceived emotion is so individual that that the predictability of individual response is impossible to determine. Viewers with differing experience and biases interpret expression as significantly different in both meaning and intensity. Speakers work to avoid viewer perceptions of excessive or inappropriate emotion resulting from personal context and allow individual perception to occur in a more balanced fashion, amplifying the presented narrative as the key thematic element. FaceReader automatically analyzes facial expressions, providing users with an objective assessment of a person's emotional expression. With the newest algorithms and technology, FaceReader will offer high-speed scanning, allowing effective analysis in all situations with 90% accuracy.

THE FUTURE OF FACIAL RECOGNITION TECHNOLOGY

The evolution of FRT over the last 50 years has given us the capacity to examine emotion in an entirely new way. For many and perhaps most Americans, emotional perception and response are most commonly spontaneous and reactive. We act toward and react to each other with a minimally defined vocabulary of expression and lack both understanding and fluency in emotional communication. As we move forward, beginning with our leaders, the development of a conscious and deliberate ability to express feelings and evoke positive and supportive responses will become a part of American political life. As with every other aspect of politics, new discoveries and techniques will be discussed and evaluated in the numerous venues of modern media. Beginning with an understanding of facial expression and its relationship to felt and perceived emotion, we can anticipate the development of a physiologically based common language of expression. Just as identical musculature of expression indicates identical emotion, but may have a different value for individuals in different cultures, the research discussed identifies these same phenomena within our American culture, noting for example differing qualitative responses to the perception of anger.

As the examination of emotion and its role in communication advances, we are likely to develop an increasingly comprehensive understanding of how facial expression and emotion can be used together to improve communication. This will require the development of a corresponding emotional vocabulary. As researchers and political analysts improve their understanding of emotional perception and its impact in political process, their discoveries will inform people at all levels of political interaction. I hold no doubt that the same efficacy that is so sought after in politics will be equally pursued in business and education. From there perhaps therapeutic and rehabilitative enterprises will adapt these new capacities to their own uses in medical and correctional environments.

We are in a period of profound economic and social change. Advances in the speed and capacities of electronic media are changing the way we work and the ways we communicate with one another. We are rapidly adding to the visual component of remote communication. Skype, Facetime, and video-conferencing are becoming increasingly common, and high-definition television and video are making our electronic interactions increasingly vivid. As we develop an ever larger video footprint, we will learn to communicate with increasing sophistication. While we have historically participated in political interaction and sought to evaluate our leaders as passive viewers of increasingly opinionated information, we will soon have the ability to access evaluations from the analyses of material in the C-SPAN Video Library. C-SPAN's records are the vanguard of a new level of information and the basis for an unprecedented ability for research. They open the possibility of new and expanded research into emotion in political communication.

CHAPTER 9

A SOCIAL PRACTICE CAPITAL TO ENHANCE THE C-SPAN ARCHIVES TO SUPPORT PUBLIC AFFAIRS PROGRAMMING

Sorin Adam Matei, Purdue University

Digitization of media content represents a boon for research. Digital media content can be envisaged as more than stories or images; it can be imagined as easily as a record of human behavior, which can be analyzed quantitatively or qualitatively. Furthermore, analysis results can be quickly and efficiently turned into measures or evaluation indicators. These can enrich the metadata associated with the original content and can be visualized online alongside the visual content. Visualization tools can help the users or analysts understand the significance of the content and of the social context that led to its production or that shapes its consequences. Seen from this perspective, if sufficiently large, any digital media repository, of any kind, can be considered a potential "big dataset." In what follows I will argue that the C-SPAN Archives' unique holdings of public debates can be treated as "big data" that can support a very productive social scientific agenda. In addition, the products of such research can be used for enhancing the way the information is presented, searched, or used on the C-SPAN Video Library site (http://www.c-span.org). Later in this chapter I will advocate for utilizing a programmatic strategy to extend the data capabilities of the C-SPAN Archives to serve journalists and decision makers in a new and more productive way. Specifically, I will propose that metadata generated through social scientific research can be used for discovering important nodes of debate, in the C-SPAN records, both at the semantic and interactional/actor level, which can be further employed as resources for data-driven journalism or evidence-based policy research.

My observations are focused mostly on the public debates captured by the C-SPAN Archives, be they congressional or electoral. However, once the case is made for utilizing the proposed methodology for connecting content and media actors in a network of interaction, the method can be extended to other types of C-SPAN, or more generally public affairs, content.

THEORETICAL APPROACHES TO ANALYZING PUBLIC AFFAIRS VIDEO CONTENT

The Debate Network Approach

A good part of the C-SPAN Video Library captures what was said, to whom, and when in regard to a specific topic of public interest. Committee hearings, floor debates, and electoral speeches or debates are types of public discourse in which narrative and argument are constructed and addressed to a specific person or audience. Such narratives should not be seen as insulated exchanges between pairs of senders-receivers. They are usually long strings of conversations, in which speakers become listeners, taking alternate turns in the conversation. Furthermore, as actors participate in multiple conversations, these longer chains of interaction intersect with each other, forming a network of debate. In all truth, just like in genealogy, if you go deep enough, everybody is connected with everybody else in the public sphere. However, not everyone talks equally to everyone. The generalized network of conversation contains distinct subnetworks defined by topic, occasion, time, affiliations, and so on. Subnetworks are connected by bridge-makers, topic, and actors, who become the hinge linkages in any debate.

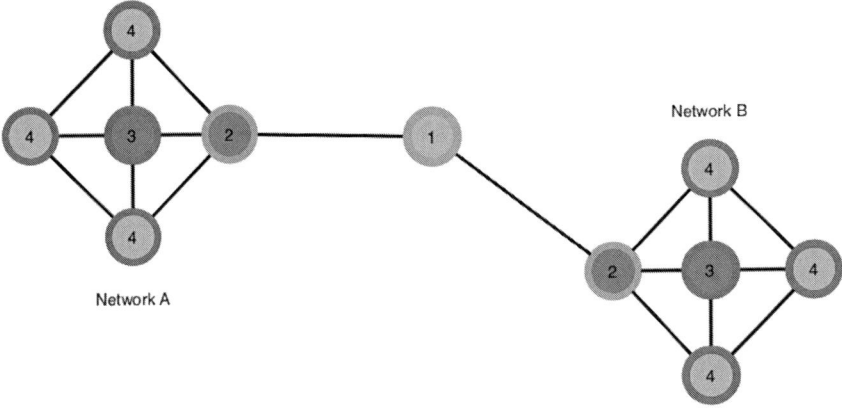

Figure 9.1 A hypothetical communication/interaction network made of two subnetworks, A and B.

Determining an actor's impact on any debate network, especially his or her potential to serve as a hinge, requires, however, careful consideration. Since the data under scrutiny are linked data, their main characteristic is not only the amount of what was said. It is also equally if even not more important to determine who has said what to whom. In other words, network location is just as important as the amount of contribution to a network of debate. Network location can make the communication of some individuals influential, even if they do not say a lot. For example, if we have a simple network of communication between 10 actors, as in Figure 9.1, and the lines represent a one-time, two-way conversation of equal weight, it appears that actors A3 and B3 (located at the center of Networks A and B) are the most important, since they have the most numerous links. However, if we remove either of them from the network, the communication processes between the other nodes remain relative unchanged. Everybody will be connected to everybody else directly or indirectly and in about the same amounts. The communication process can continue unabated, such as that A4 is still part of the same network of debate as B4. However, if we remove actor 1 from the network, although she is the lowest connected and least "vocal" member of the network, communicating only with two other network members, the overall network unravels. None of the members of Network A can now talk with any member of Network B.

The importance of strategically placed nodes, like Node 1, is not only of theoretical importance. There are, in fact, several empirical measures that capture the relative ranking of all nodes in a network as a function of their ability to connect other nodes to each other. One of these measures is betweenness centrality (Freeman, 1977), which indicates how often a node is on the shortest paths between all the other nodes in the network. Another way to describe the measure is to say that in any network the central nodes are those that lie on a high proportion of paths between other nodes in the network. The measure itself is expressed as a proportion, allowing comparisons between nodes and between networks. Returning to the example presented in Figure 9.1, it becomes immediately apparent that Node 1 is the one that is most frequently on the shortest path between all the other nodes, although it only has two direct links of its own to two other nodes.

Betweenness centrality has been proposed by Freeman (1977) with the specific intent to measure communication flows. Later work has adapted the measure to capture a more subtle conceptual relationship—namely, that of social capital (Li, Liao, & Yen, 2013). It is apparent that those nodes that are most central in a network are those that can call upon the broadest and farthest reaching communicative and other resources. This perspective is rooted in the work of Bourdieu (1986), one of the creators of the term, who proposed that social capital is "the aggregate of the actual or potential resources which are linked to possession of a durable network of more or less institutionalized relationships of mutual acquaintance and recognition" (p. 249).

The Practice Capital Approach

The twin concepts of betweenness centrality and social capital can be applied to debate and communication networks if we consider any given debate as a particular type of social practice. Multimodal, pluri-actor debates are dominated by the actors that say the right things at the right time, not by the ones who talk all the time. The centrality of an utterance is in fact determined by the centrality of the actor who makes it the communication network. Given, however, that in a debate the social interaction and the social capital derived from it are a function of taking a turn of speech at the right moment, it is not who you talk to in a directive way, but what part of the *topic* you address and where in the conversation your utterance fits in. In consequence, we need to redefine the concept of social capital when applied to generalized debates and conversations by projecting it through a *practice* lens. A debate is a series of arguments about a topic. It is a hortatory social practice. Talking to other members of the debate is not as important as engaging the topic at the central point of the debate to practically change opinions or a state of fact. Finding the right moment to say something is a particular *phronesis* (practical reason) skill, which is a core component of any rhetorical and, some might say, social practice (Flyvbjerg, 2001; Geertz, 2001). Practice in this context entails all the activities of all the actors engaged in a debate, regardless of whether they address each other directly or not. The practice space of a debate is similar to a work site. It is not necessary for the work to progress that the workers talk to each other. What is important is that the workers do their job and participate as much as they can in the activities required by their building project.

In conclusion, I propose to explore the C-SPAN debates through a practice capital lens to

- map the networks of debate surrounding a specific topic to define a practice space;
- define, measure, and visualize the level of centrality of the actors participating in these networks;
- identify the leaders of such networks;
- visualize their positions in a practice space; and
- make the data available to journalists, policymakers, and other interested researchers and practitioners.

A METHODOLOGY TO ANALYZE AND VISUALIZE C-SPAN METADATA

In what follows I will present a proof of concept analysis of a given debate and a possible method for using the data thus gleaned to improve the search capabilities of the C-SPAN Archives. Later in this chapter I will propose an environment for data journalism that would make the C-SPAN Archives a leader in the dissemination of open source big data for public affairs analysis.

To illustrate the feasibility and utility of using a practice capital theoretical lens in visualizing and analyzing the C-SPAN Archives data, I utilize in a proof of concept analysis a very small subsample of information available through C-SPAN.org. I chose a recent congressional debate of notoriety, listed in the C-SPAN Video Library as "popular," namely, the Joint Select Committee on Deficit Reduction Hearings (Joint Select Committee, 2011). I also considered this debate as particularly fit for demonstrating the practice capital concept because the hearings are somewhat scripted and the sequences are controlled by a given schedule and topic, so the arguments are structured into a broader debate at a more abstract level. While the speakers address each other and the public in attendance, their real aim is to move present and future public opinion. Speakers participate in the oratorical practice of communicating across the immediate boundaries of the time and space of their utterances; they construct a space of debate where specific interventions will be considered more or less important by the degree of centrality of a given speaker's insertion in the conversation by addressing the core issues of the topic. Those who communicate in *media res*, in the middle of the debate, and who address the most important aspect of the debate, will by necessity be considered the more central, regardless of the amount of time they spend talking.

Applying these theoretical and methodological criteria to the problem at hand, we analyzed the hearings that took place on October 26 and November 1, 2011. The debates included 17 different speakers, some committee members, and some witnesses, lasting 280 minutes, or over 4 hours. There were 115 turns of speech, as defined by C-SPAN, which attributed each speaker a specific time slot based on significance and length of intervention.

We connected each speaker to other speakers using a "gravitational pull" algorithm. The strength of the ties was defined by the formula $Ts_1 * Ts_2 / d^2$, where Ts_x is the time spent talking by a given user and d is the distance in terms of turns of speech between speakers. The formula and the software code was created for the Visible Effort and KredibleNet projects (Matei et al., 2014), which aim to map the network of interactions between Wikipedia editors, which are similarly sequential and are part of a "practice" space of knowledge construction. The formula presents a certain advantage: it exponentially decays the strength of the link between speakers as they speak at greater intervals from each other. For example, if two speakers speak for 10 minutes in

A Social Practice Capital to Enhance the C-SPAN Archives to Support Public Affairs Programming   CHAPTER 9   115

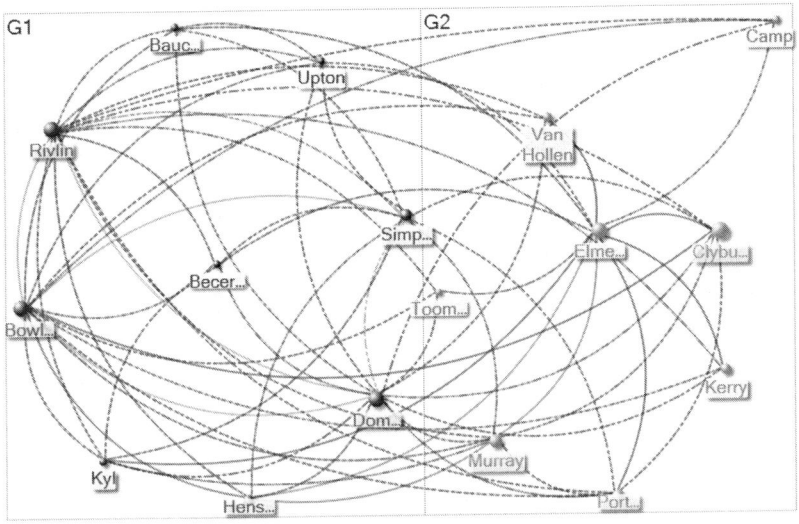

Figure 9.2 Network of debate, October and November 2011 deficit reduction hearings. Larger dots represent higher levels of centrality.

succession, their link will have a value of 100 conventional units. If the speakers speak the same 10 minutes each, but at an interval of 10 turns of speech, their link will be 100 times weaker, having a value of 1 conventional unit.

The gravitational model avoids producing a saturated network of identical links, in which everybody is connected with everybody else at the same level of intensity. Our gravitational formula desaturates the network by connecting specific pairs across practice spaces and individualizes the ties ty assigning each of them a specific weight.

Since mapping the relationships in the C-SPAN conversations start with an individual debate, links across debates are summed for all pairs of speakers that can be found in both debates. The final network of interactions is presented in Figure 9.2.

As expected, given the multiplicity of interventions, amounting to an average of 6.7 turns per speaker, at first scrutiny there is a profusion of linkages between talkers, with no obvious leader. However, if we focus not on the number of connections between users, which represent the rhetorical practice connections between users, but on their level of centrality, as defined by the shortest paths between the other speakers that go through them, we would be able to

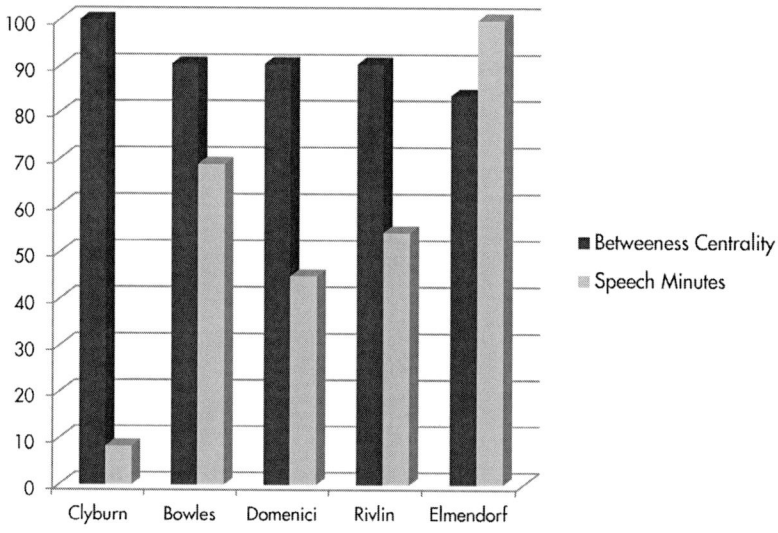

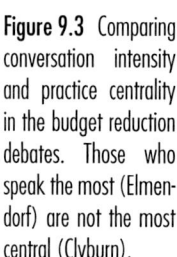

Figure 9.3 Comparing conversation intensity and practice centrality in the budget reduction debates. Those who speak the most (Elmendorf) are not the most central (Clyburn).

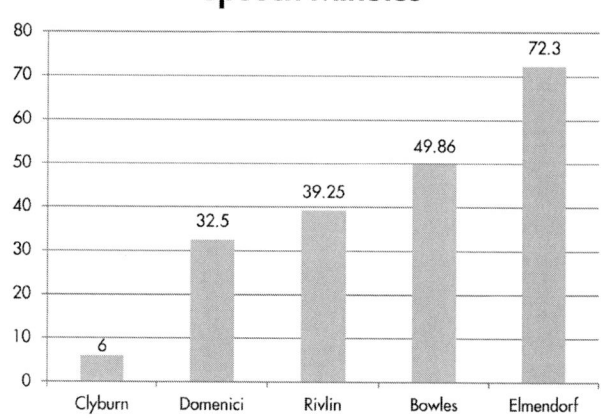

pick some clear leaders. These leaders are represented in Figure 9.2 by the size of the dots, calculated using the NodeXL software (Hansen, Schneiderman, & Smith, 2010). We notice that nodes such as Rivlin, Elmendorf, and Clyburn are much larger than the others nodes. This means that these speakers took turns of speech in the middle of the debate and their level of oratorical practice is much higher than that of the other speakers. Figure 9.3 summarizes the distinction between the amount of raw contributions (in minutes spoken) and the centrality of intervention, as defined by a network analysis of betweenness centrality. Figure 9.3 indicates that the top talkers in terms of minutes (normalized by the value of the most verbose talker) are not the same ones that are most central (normalized by the centrality of the most central speaker). Specifically, while the most present speaker was unsurprisingly the main witness, Douglas Elmendorf, the director of the Congressional Budget Office, who spoke for a total of 72 minutes, the most centrally positioned was the congressman of South Carolina, William Clyburn, who spoke for only 6 minutes. However, the congressman spoke right in the middle of both sessions, asking core questions about income equality and the impact of budget reduction on various social income groups, which sparked further and lively debates.

APPLYING THE RESULTS OF PRACTICE CAPITAL ANALYSIS: VISUALIZATIONS AND DATA JOURNALISM APPLICATION PROGRAMMING INTERFACE

The example presented in the previous section illustrates the research promises of network and practice capital analysis applied to public affairs video data. However, how can the results of such analysis be applied in a concrete manner, and what intellectual and practical benefits can be derived from this application? In essence, I propose two core strategies. One involves creating data visualization and selection/search criteria embedded on the C-SPAN Video Library site to allow an at-a-glance understanding of who leads, dominates, or may sway a debate. The visualization cues can also be used for searching the site for individuals that meet certain criteria of debate performance or importance. The other strategy involves enhancing the search and information delivery application programming interface (API) of the C-SPAN Video Library in such a way that other computers or services can retrieve information from C-SPAN databases directly. Network and debate performance can thus be automatically exported, imported, reprocessed, and visualized by third-party applications. Such applications, similar to Facebook apps, would reside on third-party sites and would support data visualization and analysis for data journalism projects.

Figure 9.4 illustrates how the current C-SPAN search pages can be enhanced with visualization tools that enrich the media experience and viewer understanding of public affairs debates.

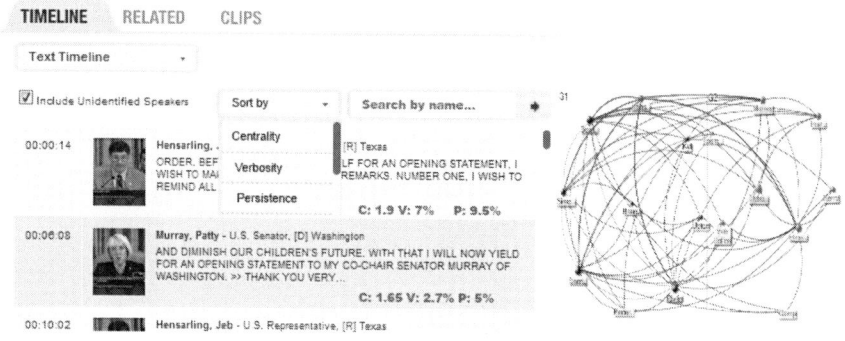

Figure 9.4 Proposed interface for sorting and searching for speakers on the C-SPAN Video Library site.

Using as a specific example the same October and November 2011 deficit reduction hearings depicted in Figure 9.2, I have added new sorting, searching, and visualizing tools to an interface mock-up. For example, we added a drop-down box labeled "Sort by" which allows the reader to bring to the top of the list of speakers (currently ordered in simple chronological order) the individuals that dominated the debates in three different ways: by centrality, verbosity, and persistence. Once ordered, each speaker entry will display at the bottom as normalized measures between 0% and 100% as indicators of centrality, verbosity, and persistence. Centrality is the core measure, which indicates what proportion of shortest paths between the other debate participants pass through that given speaker. When centrality is 100%, all of the shortest conversation paths go through that speaker. Verbosity is the proportion of all the debate time accounted by the speaker, while persistence is proportion of turns of speech accounted by the speaker. In addition, a clickable network graph, whose nodes increase in size with centrality, visualizes the network of communication. When a node is clicked, it and its entire constellation of direct connections are highlighted in red. The highlighted area can be then investigated by clicking the neighboring nodes or by generating summary statistics for that subgroup.

The second strategy for leveraging the C-SPAN Video Library holdings to create new opportunities for research and public use involves extending the capabilities of the Video Library database to include data services that can allow third-party applications to create their own analyses, infographics, and visualizations. This strategy aims to turn the Archives into a data journalism hub of information and into a leader in the field of serving the public interest with new and relevant sources of information that can shape not only public conversations but also public policy and affairs more broadly.

The idea of extending the database API to allow third-party developers to use the rich C-SPAN Video Library metadata is inspired by Web 2.0 design principles (O'Reilly, 2005; Shelly & Frydenberg, 2010), which have already migrated to governmental and public affairs websites, such as data.gov. The fundamental idea is to extract valuable metadata from the archive repositories using methods such as the ones suggested above, whereby speakers or political actors are given scores of centrality, verbosity, or persistence for one or multiple debates. The metadata is stored in the C-SPAN Video Library alongside other types of information (e.g., speaker name, official title, dates of debate, specific speech information). The open API policy would create a method of querying the database by other computers via a Web page request. When a specific URL is requested by a third-party site, such as *The New York Times*, the C-SPAN Video Library returns not a page or a video but a stream of information relevant to the search. For example, a search for "Centrality>10, Dec 10–21 2007, healthcare" would return a list of speakers in a computer readable format (XML or JSON) that have a centrality of at least 10 in debates that match the keyword *healthcare*. For each speaker there will be other types of metadata in addition to centrality, such as the district he or she represents, official position or title, and so forth. The data can then be easily plotted by the third-party site as new charts, maps, or networks. These artifacts can be used to illustrate Web-published material or as evidentiary materials for policy papers.

CONCLUSION

In this chapter I have proposed a suite of strategies for redefining the use of the video records archived by the C-SPAN Archives, especially those that refer to public affairs debates. Inspired by a social capital approach adapted as a practice capital lens, I propose that the turns of speech identifiable in the C-SPAN Video Library recordings can be used to build a network of oratorical practices. Such networks represent the social infrastructure of any given debate. They reflect the natural division of labor in the practice of argumentation and debate surrounding any given issue. Within this division of labor, some actors (speakers) are considered to be more or less important, not as a function of how much they said, but of what, when, and to which audience (local or generalized) they said it. I take the social network analysis approach that the speakers who are most central, who minimize the paths between the other speakers, are the most important. Centrality is measured as the degree to which a conversation will unravel if a specific speaker is removed.

Determining centrality is a first step toward visualizing the structure of the conversation and pinpointing the most important speakers. Once identified, this information can be visualized by the general or specialized public, either for personal edification or for generating evidence and analyses for journalistic or policy projects. The latter activity would situate the C-SPAN Archives at the forefront of the interactive, open API revolution, which empowers consumers to become producers of new information and insights.

My proposal is in fact to push the C-SPAN Video Library to become a one-stop destination of choice for all those interested in quantitative answers to the core questions that characterize any public affairs debate: Who said, what, to whom, and when? Of course, the aim of facilitating answers to these questions is not a goal in and of itself. The goal is to help the users form new answers to the more important question: Why? These answers will enrich our knowledge about any given topic. Through them, the C-SPAN Video Library will become a powerful resource for furthering one of the most cherished values of the C-SPAN project: to create a better informed citizenry.

PART IV

TEACHING CASE STUDIES

CHAPTER **10**

USING THE C-SPAN ARCHIVES TO TEACH MASS COMMUNICATION THEORY

Glenn G. Sparks, Purdue University

Many of the other chapters in this volume illustrate the truth of what scholars assume about the C-SPAN Video Library (http://www.c-span.org): it is an invaluable resource for the study of numerous historical events and is a virtual treasure trove for scholars, students, and laypeople alike as they seek to study and review key speeches, events, committee hearings, congressional sessions, and so forth. Although this assumption is certainly true, the C-SPAN Archives represents a much broader resource than most scholars probably realize. Indeed, even among communication scholars, the C-SPAN Archives is associated almost exclusively with the study of American history and politics. My purpose in this chapter is to expand the boundaries of that traditional association by illustrating the value of the Archives for teaching the course in mass communication theory. Given my own experience in using the Archives for this purpose, I have no doubt that other teachers in this area will conclude that the C-SPAN Video Library ought to become a regular feature in their course curricula. Moreover, although my focus in this chapter is upon the application of the archives to theory in mass communication, it seems evident from my experience that the Archives holds promise for playing an essential pedagogical role in many other course curricula that go well beyond the walls of traditional courses in history and political science.

My purpose in the remainder of this chapter is fivefold: (1) to provide a brief description of the course in mass communication theory in which I employ regular use of the C-SPAN Archives, (2) to explicate the specific elements that the Archives contributes to the effective teaching of this course, (3) to provide a brief overview of three specific videos from the Archives that I integrate into the course, (4) to provide details on a specific assignment for the undergraduate student that can be used effectively in teaching the course, and (5) to outline possible future directions in my own use of the Archives in teaching the course in mass communication theory.

THE COURSE IN MASS COMMUNICATION THEORY

I teach a course at Purdue University in the Brian Lamb School of Communication that is titled Theories of Mass Communication (COM 33000). The course is designed for students who have already qualified for the major in communication by successfully passing three preliminary courses with a minimum average of "B." Consequently, the course draws enrollment primarily from undergraduates in their third and fourth years of study—and mainly from those who have declared mass communication as their area of concentration in the major. The course enrolls 25 students per semester and is taught twice during the academic year. Because of the diverse nature of theoretical perspectives in mass communication and my own general expertise in the area of scientific theory, I introduce students in the first two weeks to the sorts of questions that scholars address in each of the scientific, normative, and critical theoretical traditions but devote the remainder of the semester to theory and research in the scientific vein. Over 15 years ago, I decided to write a text book for this course after feeling unhappy with the available options on the market. The first edition of *Mass Communication Research: A Basic Overview* was published by

Wadsworth in 2002 and it is now in its fourth edition (Sparks, 2013). After a brief introduction to theory and method, the text includes chapters on the history of research in mass communication and the time people spend with media. Subsequent chapters are devoted to theory and research in each of the following areas: media violence, sexual content in media, emotional reactions to media, persuasion, news and politics, stereotyping, new technology, and the theory of Marshall McLuhan.

The purpose of this class is to provide students with a rigorous exploration of the diverse theories and concepts that have guided research in mass communication. In addition, it seeks to provide an understanding of the research associated with the theories and acquaints them with the individual theorists who are responsible for the key theoretical ideas. In addition, it seeks to familiarize students with issues of public policy and controversy that revolve around some of the key theoretical areas and research studies covered in the course. While the pedagogical application that I make with the C-SPAN Archives is specific to the purposes of this course, it should be clear that there is considerable potential held by the Archives to make contributions to other courses on mass communication that may be structured differently.

WHAT DO THE ARCHIVES CONTRIBUTE?

For the purposes of teaching the theory course in mass communication, the C-SPAN Archives makes three special contributions. First, the Archives helps to defeat a tendency for students to treat theoretical ideas as a sort of received wisdom that functions as something distinct from particular individuals. One concept that I attempt to convey to students is that theorists are people who literally make up ideas that seem helpful in understanding a given phenomenon. Reading about a theorist and hearing a professor talk about a theorist's ideas is a poor substitute compared to encountering the theorist directly in a video. In the case of mass communication theorists, students are able to see and hear exactly how a theorist articulates a position and engages an audience. There is hardly anything, short of introducing a theorist in person to the class (an extremely rare opportunity), that humanizes the scholar to students more than a video presentation that features that person talking. It is one of the most powerful ways to bring theory to life that teachers can possibly employ in the classroom setting.

Second, students who are able to encounter a theorist through the Video Library gain a dimension of understanding about that person that exceeds anything that can be captured in either the reading material or a standard course lecture. In addition to the simple appreciation that the theorist is actually a real person, there is much insight to be gained by listening to and observing the speaker's cadence, emotional tone, facial expressions, gestures, and lexical choices. As a result of watching a theorist in a video clip, students will often be able to gain an appreciation for a theorist's personality and his or her general emotional disposition. This appreciation often permits students to draw connections between the particulars of a theory and the personality of a theorist. For example, it may be easier to understand why a theorist is so adamant about a particular theoretical point upon observing his or her precision in language, emotional passion, and confident tone.

Third, the C-SPAN Archives affords students the opportunity to see theorists talking about their own ideas and applying them in a context that is typically quite different from the standard academic setting. Often, the theorists are providing testimony on an issue related to public policy. As such, students are able to enrich their understanding of a theory by going beyond the formal theoretical points and getting the chance to see how a theorist relates those points to particular issues and problems and communicates with different audiences. The result of this sort of encounter is a much richer grasp than an instructor can provide of how the original theorist thinks about the importance and application of his or her own ideas.

THREE SPECIFIC EXAMPLES

Tom Wolfe on Marshall McLuhan

In 1999, the author Tom Wolfe was invited to Fordham University to give a lecture on Marshall McLuhan (see Figure 10.1). The entire lecture can be found in the C-SPAN Video Library by searching on McLuhan's name (Wolfe, 1999). McLuhan had died nearly 20 years earlier, but his legacy as an insightful

Using the C-SPAN Archives to Teach Mass Communication Theory **CHAPTER 10** 127

Figure 10.1 Tom Wolfe lectures on Marshall McLuhan in 1999. (From Wolfe, 1999. © 1999 by C-SPAN.)

thinker about the new era of electronic media had only grown stronger. It has continued to grow since 1999, and this is the main reason that I include an entire chapter on McLuhan's ideas at the end of my text. The lecture by Wolfe is just over an hour. The entire lecture can be assigned to students for viewing and study and is useful because it provides a compelling example of a non-academic who has thought deeply about McLuhan's ideas, knew McLuhan personally, and shares stories about McLuhan that only he could share and are not available anywhere else. Overall, the impact of this video is to provide a first-person account of McLuhan that gives students a unique glimpse into his mind and his personality.

It is worth mentioning that some of Wolfe's comments in this lecture as well as the stories that he recounts from even earlier years do reflect the fact that culture has changed in the interim. For example, he opens the lecture by remembering the time in the 1970s when he took McLuhan to a topless restaurant in San Francisco for lunch. The way in which Wolfe tells this tale was certainly meant to be "entertaining" to his audience but may strike many in the current culture as chauvinistic and demeaning to women (Wolfe, 1999). This aspect of the video can be used to bring students' attention to changing cultural norms in this area. Despite some discomfort with this aspect of the lecture, the stories he tells hold genuine insights into

128 PART IV Teaching Case Studies

Figure 10.2 Joanne Cantor testifies about TV ratings in 1997. (From Cantor, 1997. © 1997 by C-SPAN.)

the way McLuhan's mind worked and promote deeper understanding of his perspective.

Joanne Cantor on Television Ratings

On February 27, 1997, the U.S. Senate Committee on Commerce, Science, and Transportation held hearings which lasted nearly four hours on the new television rating system that was patterned after the MPAA movie rating system and adopted as the new industry standard. The entire hearing is in the C-SPAN Archives (Cantor, 1997). In addition to testimony from Jack Valenti, who was the head of the MPAA at the time, the hearings contained a seven-minute statement from Professor Joanne Cantor (the statement begins at 3:13:55). Insofar as Cantor is one of the leading researchers and theorists in mass communication, this hearing (and especially her testimony) provide a unique opportunity for students to see her giving an important statement on a practical policy issue that arises in the context of the theory course. Cantor's statement (see Figure 10.2) is a comprehensive and persuasive summary of her own research and the research of other scholars that led her to state unequivocally that the new television rating system is not only "not helpful" but constitutes a "giant step backward" (Cantor, 1997).

One of the valuable features of this video example in teaching the theory course is that Cantor demonstrates the relationship between theory, research, and practice. Often the course in mass communication theory can seem dry, abstract, and conceptual. This clip shows students that the theories about the effects of media messages that guide research also have clear practical significance in the arena of policy discussion and implementation. The clip also raises interesting questions that can be explored in class discussion about the lack of influence that scholars seem to have on issues of public policy. At the end of the clip, Cantor notes that she, along with virtually every media researcher who attended earlier meetings with the ratings implementation group, recommended that the proposed system be scrapped. As she also notes that recommendation "obviously . . . fell on deaf ears" (Cantor, 1997). This fact raises a significant problem that students can ponder and for which they can be encouraged to brainstorm potential solutions.

Edward Donnerstein on Media Violence

On October 20, 1993, the U.S. Senate Committee on Commerce, Science, and Transportation held hearings on violence in television programs. The hearings included testimony that went for over four and one-half hours, and the entire session is in the C-SPAN archives (Donnerstein, 1993). Nearly two and one-half hours into the session (2:28:10), Edward Donnerstein began to testify on the theory, research results, and implications of studies on media violence (see Figure 10.3, p. 130). Once again, students have an opportunity in studying this video to see one of the leading scholars in the area of media violence provide a succinct summary of the role that media play in contributing to violence in society.

In addition to the general advantages that students gain upon seeing one of the theorists mentioned prominently in the mass communication theory course, this example is particularly powerful because of a general attitude prevalent among many undergraduates upon their first encounter with the literature on media violence. Based on their own personal experience, the typical attitude expressed by many undergraduates is that media violence is not a significant contributor to violence in real life. They

Figure 10.3 Ed Donnerstein testifies on media violence in 1993. (From Donnerstein, 1993. © 1993 by C-SPAN.)

tend to reason that since they have consumed copious amounts of media violence during their lifetime and live nonaggressive lives, the supposed link between consuming media violence and aggression must be exaggerated. Given the opportunity to see how confidently and succinctly Donnerstein (1993) summarizes the evidence, I have found this video clip to be quite useful in encouraging students to rethink their understanding about how media violence can affect aggressive behavior. Not only does this clip present a close encounter with a media theorist; it also has the capacity to change what students believe about the role that media play in their own lives. This is one of the key goals in many courses in mass communication theory.

A SPECIFIC ASSIGNMENT BASED ON THE C-SPAN ARCHIVES

In addition to using videos from the C-SPAN Archives to enhance instruction, students can be encouraged to navigate their own way through the archived material and study particular examples that pertain to course content. To facilitate this process, I developed a very simple assignment that requires students to search the C-SPAN Video Library, identify a video that is relevant to the course, provide abstracting information about the video, and identify something new learned as a result of studying the material. An example of a completed assignment that can be used to illustrate the requirements for students is shown in Figure 10.4 (p. 132).

One particular advantage of this assignment that goes beyond the material to be learned from a specific video is the awareness that students develop about the existence of the C-SPAN archives and their potential for discovering information that may be pertinent to a host of topics and course content across the entire academic curriculum. At the Brian Lamb School of Communication at Purdue, this is an important advantage that faculty want to exploit as part of our students' basic experience. However, given the incredible resource material held in the Archives, this is a feasible goal worthy of any course in communication at any institution.

FUTURE DIRECTIONS

In future semesters, I anticipate that my own use of the C-SPAN Archives will blossom into new pedagogical directions. Specifically, an obvious extension of the basic assignment illustrated in Figure 10.4 is to ask students to create a video project or report that incorporates appropriate clips from the Archives that make essential points related to mass communication theory. Given the volume of material in the Archives related to mass communication theory, it even seems possible to contemplate structuring a mini-unit or short-course curriculum that is structured around archived material. I am hopeful that this chapter will serve to stimulate such efforts so that students around the world can become accustomed to using the C-SPAN Archives routinely to enhance their education.

C-SPAN ARCHIVES ASSIGNMENT — COM 33000

Your Name Here

Section I
1. Title of the video clip: Understanding Violent Children
2. Date of the event: April 28, 1998
3. Name of the speaker(s): Joanne Cantor (Professor, University of Wisconsin–Madison)
4. Length of the event: 2 hours, 30 minutes

Section II
1. General topic in the course related to the video: Social learning theory (media effects).
2. Summary of the video clip: This video clip was part of hearings held by the House Committee on Education and the Workforce (Early Childhood, Youth & Families). The focus of the testimony was on the reasons children become violent, as well as the strategies that might be used to prevent violent behavior. Prof. Cantor focused on exposure to media violence as a cause of children's aggressive behavior. She summarized the research evidence and the strong consensus that exists on the notion that exposure to media violence is unhealthy and produces violent behavior. She also fielded a number of questions about the research and about efforts to increase media literacy among parents and children in order to reduce the effects of media violence on aggressive behavior.
3. What *new* thing I learned from this video clip that concerns communication theory: Prof. Cantor said several things that were new to me that didn't seem to be covered in either the text discussion or the class discussion. First, in over 40% of violent TV episodes, the bad violent characters are never punished. Second, only 4% of violent TV programs contain a theme that promotes nonviolence. According to the theory of social learning, it would seem that these facts might mean that TV programs could increase imitation of violent acts. Finally, Cantor said that there had been no major research study to compare different approaches to promoting critical learning skills.
4. Precise time interval of the video clip: Cantor's precise testimony began at 52 minutes, 10 seconds. She concluded her statement at 58 minutes, 24 seconds. She then responded to questions from the Committee members—particularly at the 1 hour, 23 minute mark of the hearings.

Figure 10.4   Course assignment to facilitate research in the C-SPAN Archives.

CHAPTER 11

TEACHING AMERICAN GOVERNMENT CONCEPTS USING C-SPAN

Robert X. Browning, Purdue University and C-SPAN Archives

C-SPAN videos offer excellent opportunities to introduce students to concepts and processes in American government and communication. They allow students to see the ideas presented in lectures firsthand, with real examples. These examples tend to have a lasting impact on students who have been raised on video. Examples can be used directly in lectures or in exercises that the students work through on their own.

The C-SPAN Video Library (http://www.c-span.org) has a clipping feature that allows professors to select clips that can be extracted and used in place of the entire video. These clips are short portions that can be saved for use repeatedly. The clipping feature allows one to set a begin and an end point, to name the clip, and to save it in his or her MyC-SPAN account. By saving it to a personal account, the clips are kept indexed and available for subsequent use and sharing.

Once a clip has been created and selected, it is available for use in class. There are two ways that one might consider using a clip. The first is to download it directly into a presentation. The second is to show it directly from the C-SPAN Video Library through a link that is accessed across the Internet. The first method requires a few steps and the payment of a small fee to download the video; the second method is free and easy. The first method plays faster and can easily be incorporated into presentations; the second method, using the link, can also be incorporated in any software in which an HTML link can be used.

Once a clip is selected, the share button will reveal a URL that can easily be inserted into a text document or even a PowerPoint presentation. This URL is permanent, which means that it will last from semester to semester and year to year. Clips in the Video Library are all also permanent, which means that they are never deleted. These links are to videos that remain on the C-SPAN Video Library servers.

In order to download a clip, one has to click on the purchase button. The video is moved from the Archives' servers to the user's local machine. Once the video is on the local machine, it can be used in multiple presentations. If incorporated into a PowerPoint presentation, it becomes a part of that presentation.

ILLUSTRATING THE CONCEPT OF PARTY IDENTIFICATION

One concept that we study in all American government classes is party identification. This concept is often a difficult one for students to understand since it is only measurable through survey instruments and only observable through political behavior. We usually teach that party identification

- is a learned sociopsychological attribute;
- grows stronger with age;
- influences vote choice; and
- is a low-information voting cue.

These are easily said by the instructor and memorized by the student, but the question remains whether the student really understands what the concept means. In order to drive home the meaning of the concept, the class presentation can be combined with a video illustration from the C-SPAN Video Library.

In 1990, a candidate was campaigning in the Republican primary to become a member of Congress. Republican candidate Ernest Istook was going store-to-store in an Oklahoma strip shopping center seeking votes to challenge Rep. Mickey Edwards (R-OK). Edwards was a member of the Republican leadership but had recently been caught up in the 1990 House banking scandal where some members received interest-free overdraft advances on their accounts. These had the effect of being interest-free loans that increased their pay since the overdrafts were allowed to continue somewhat indefinitely. Edwards was one of the members with overdrafts.

Since it was a primary election, only Republicans could vote for Istook or Edwards, so Istook faced the daunting task of finding registered Republicans in his retail campaigning. We pick up the video when Istook enters a Radio Shack store with the country music blaring. There he finds a young clerk showing an older gentleman the choice of telephones. (See Figure 11.1, p. 136.)

After waiting a bit, he gives a brochure to the clerk, who admits to "not being for Mickey." He then offers a brochure to the elderly customer looking at phones. The man stares at the brochure and says to Istook, "What are you?" Once he determines Istook's party, he quickly looks away and returns to phone shopping. Istook recognizes this and says, "Oh, you are Democrat. I will give you one for November." The man responds, "Couldn't use it. You are wasting your time" (Istook, 1992).

Students quickly understand what they see. Here all the points about party identification can be understood. They see an elderly gentlemen whose party identification had clearly grown stronger with age and serves as a low-information voting cue for him. It is easy to ask the students which of the points illustrated previously they recognize from the video clip. In exams and other evaluations, the students remember the clip and the concept of party identification that they observe in this video vérité campaigning.

Figure 11.1 Republican congressional primary candidate Earnest Istook campaigns in a Radio Shack store. (From Istook, 1992. © 1992 by C-SPAN.)

MEMBERS OF CONGRESS LOBBYING FOR COMMITTEE ASSIGNMENTS

Another idea that we teach in American government is how congressional committees maintain their working environments through the replacement of members by likeminded members. The committee assignments process for congressional committees is taught in many courses on American government and Congress. It is a phenomenon in which watching a video can again reinforce the ideas that otherwise can only be described. In introducing this topic, we emphasize the following points:

1. Freshmen serve apprenticeships.
2. Freshmen don't get assigned to major committees such as Appropriations.
3. Leaders seek members from safe seats, who are loyal to the party, and who are consensus builders for major committees.
4. Senior members make the assignments.
5. Members lobby senior members for assignment support.

Figure 11.2 Congressional candidate Carrie Meek meets with Rules Committee chair Rep. Joseph Moakley to lobby for a coveted committee assignment. (From Meek, 1992. © 1992 by C-SPAN.)

Following this introduction, we show a video of Carrie Meek (D-FL) going office-to-office to speak with Democratic congressional leaders to lobby for her committee assignment. Since Meek won her primary election and has no general election opponent, she is using this time to get a head start on meeting the senior members who will make the appointments. In this video, we see candidate Meek calling on House Rules Committee Chairman Rep. Joseph Moakley (D-MA), who is an ex officio member of the Democratic Steering and Policy Committee that makes the Democratic committee assignments. (See Figure 11.2.)

Rep. Moakley explores Meek's background in the Florida state legislature. He also asks her about her election percentage. He makes the point that freshmen usually don't receive appointments on major committees such as Appropriations, but comments that "with the size of the freshman class this year, who knows?" recognizing the bargaining power of a large freshman class. Upon hearing of her strong election results, he also comments that "we need members from safe seats for certain assignments." The staffer accompanying Meek makes the point that she is a consensus builder, team player, and loyal to the party (Meek, 1992). In one short clip, we can see nearly all of the points outlined about the committee assignment process.

These points made about the committee assignment process are readily enforced by the video when the students can see an incoming member of Congress making the rounds lobbying for committee assignments and a committee chairman making the points of the lecture. Students understand the points when they can see them in video that reinforces the lecture.

STUDENT ASSIGNMENTS USING C-SPAN VIDEO

In addition to these classroom examples, I also use video in student assignments. Students are required to write a short paper (five to seven pages) that uses clips from the C-SPAN Video Library to illustrate a concept or process discussed in the lectures or textbooks. This assignment requires that they first research a topic in the text such as filibusters, seniority, civility, or reciprocity and then find video examples that can be used to illustrate that concept or process. This assignment is used successfully in both political science and communication classes.

Since the videos can be clipped and embedded, students are advised to create a blog using one of the free blog sites such as Tumblr or Blogger and combine their text with the embedded video clip. This technique is easier for the students than creating an HTML document. The blog software handles all of the formatting of the text and the video for the students, allowing them to focus on the content. Sometimes I require that the students also make a presentation of their work, which means that they must stand in front of the class and present their idea with a short video clip.

The students do well with this assignment. They are motivated in the assignment because they have a manageable task to research something they are interested in and then incorporate the video. They need to include three video clips in their paper. Papers have included many topics of the course, and some students have found unusual clips to illustrate their subjects.

THE VALUE OF C-SPAN VIDEOS

It is a well-worn cliché to refer to new generations of students as part of the video generation. Current students are several generations removed from the TV-saturated children schooled on Sesame Street. Nonetheless, short videos serve as an effective teaching tool in lectures and for out-of-class assignments. C-SPAN videos are unique in that they cast the professor in the role of producer and director. As producer, the professor must first decide what videos are appropriate and find those videos through the extensive C-SPAN Video Library. C-SPAN coverage includes congressional sessions, hearings, and presidential and political speeches, as well as the type of behind the scenes videos illustrated in this chapter. It can seem like a daunting task to the uninitiated, but professors often read about something that happened or by chance see a clip on another edited program, then they find the source program in the C-SPAN Video Library. Once the appropriate program is found, the professor becomes the director, using the Video Library's clipping tool to select the right clip to make the point. One question often asked is how long should a clip be. The general rule based on experience is that clips should not be longer than 3 minutes, and clips lasting about 90 seconds work best. Attention spans are limited, and long clips tend to lose students' attention. However, sometimes there is no choice but to use a longer clip in order to include both points of view, or to help students understand the issue.

The C-SPAN Video Library contains a vast array of programs that are appropriate for a wide range of courses. For political science courses, the choices may be apparent. For communication courses, the choices range from policy to behavior. One could say that all C-SPAN programming is about various forms of communication, from formal to informal, from rhetoric to spontaneous, from small group persuasion to large group speeches. C-SPAN Video Library clips add value to lectures and to assignments. They serve as a motivator both in and out of class. C-SPAN videos document primary source events, so students are not simply watching television news coverage. Rather, they are researching audio and video documents of the statements of elected and policy officials. As such it adds to the learning experience.

CHAPTER 12

INTERACTIVE LEARNING IN AND OUT OF THE CLASSROOM

Robert X. Browning, Purdue University and C-SPAN Archives

There are three programs at Purdue University that utilize the C-SPAN Archives in unique and interactive ways. One is the Purdue Institute for Civic Communication (PICC), which is directed by Carolyn Curiel, clinical professor in the Brian Lamb School of Communication at Purdue University and former U.S. ambassador. The second is a course taught by Ambassador Curiel in which C-SPAN founder and executive chairman, Brian Lamb, participates from Washington, DC. The third is a distance learning course coordinated by C-SPAN's politics senior executive producer involving three academic institutions. Each relies upon C-SPAN and its Archives in different ways.

PICC is a successor to an earlier similar program, Project IMPACT, and is now supported by funding from the Bill Daniels Fund. This program brings together students from all disciplines on campus, including engineering, the sciences, and liberal arts. It is a student-run program in which students bring leaders from media and politics to campus to take part in interactive forums. By interacting with the leaders through introductions, escorting, conducting polls, writing publicity, working with the media, and university offices, students learn valuable interpersonal and life skills that provide them both confidence and personal growth opportunities. All the while, students are learning about important policy and media questions that the forums cover. Previous guests include former Coast Guard Commandant and National Incident Commander for the 2010 *Deepwater Horizon* oil spill, Thad Allen, and also the entire panel of commentators from *Bloomberg View*, including Ezra Klein, Ramesh Ponnuru, and Margaret Carlson. In addition, there have been panels on energy and our energy future. Students researched these policies using the C-SPAN Video Library (http://www.c-span.org) in preparation for the forums.

A capstone experience for PICC is the summer maymester in Washington, DC, in which students from across campus attend a Washington seminar hosted at C-SPAN headquarters. Students visit Washington offices as well as hear speakers from a range of media, political offices, and lobby firms. On the final day, students are required to make a presentation on a policy question in which they use a video clip from the C-SPAN Video Library. Students learn how to navigate the Video Library and use video clips to make their arguments.

In addition to serving as executive director for PICC, Ambassador Carolyn Curiel also teaches a course with Brian Lamb in which guests are invited to speak to the students from Washington. These students are also required to make presentations that contain clips drawn from the C-SPAN Video Library. Students are exposed to a variety of opinion leaders and are required to prepare questions in advance and to research the guest's publications, again using the Video Library to view C-SPAN appearances.

Brian Lamb remarked that this is a new experience for him. In addressing the audience he commented that they all teach, but this is new for him to have a group of people who can give lessons in terms of what they are learning as students in a class. It is exciting for Ambassador Curiel and Brian Lamb to teach this class, but they often wonder if the students share the excitement. Brian Lamb says that you find out after the fact that the students were excited.

They now have a few people from the classes who are working at C-SPAN. One of the students is working at NBC. These are measures of success. The students talk afterward about the impact that these experiences have had on them. The perspective afforded by the Archives—being able to see people up close—provides texture to what students are learning. It has been invaluable for these instructors and students.

A similar course occurs each week hosted in the C-SPAN studios and co-ordinated by C-SPAN's politics senior executive editor, Steve Scully. Students from George Mason University, Purdue University, and the Washington Center all participate by remote links. The Purdue students connect via a distance learning room at the C-SPAN Archives. Guests include authors of books that the students are reading, which provides an opportunity for the students to ask them questions. Previous guests have included *Washington Post* reporter Dan Balz, President Carter's pollster, Pat Caddell, 1974 House Judiciary Committee member Elizabeth Holtzman, and the staff director of the Commission on Presidential Debates.

Steve Scully commented that since 2011 we have been putting the class on the air on a delayed basis because it seems silly to limit the audience to the three universities that participate. We created a website so that students can go back to view the class. Steve Scully tells the students that it's a traditional academic class with a midterm, final, papers that are due, and exam questions that often come from the guests. At the Washington Center, he meets with the students once a week for about an hour to an hour and a half with an additional lecture or a Q&A session focusing on the topic at that time.

The most recent course has focused on Congress, the media, and the presidency, so Steve Scully has been discussing different aspects of these topics with the students. The challenge is that the students at the Washington Center come from a pretty diverse background—liberal arts, history, political science, and communication—so the course is not designed for one department but for students across disciplines.

Steve Scully says that his measure of success is that students are more interested in government and politics—that they are interested in reading a newspaper or going online. He says, "I tell students that the most important title that they have is as 'citizen' and to be a good citizen is to be a consumer of news." One of the other requirements is to get a daily blog such as the *Morning Grind,* or Politico's *Playbook,* one of the free e-mail alerts that come in every morning that get students connected to Washington. They come in at the end of the semester and say that not only do they feel better educated but also that they want to continue with this process by reading a book, reading the newspaper, or going online for the news. These are the benchmarks that Steve Scully uses.

Years ago, Steve Scully was teaching a course on the presidency and politics. He brought in VHS tapes of political ads. The students could connect with the televised content and it grabbed their attention. It was the television generation and now it is the digital generation. Steve says, "You can read the book and then show the debates or ads by Obama and others and reinforce the books. Students take in the content and remember it. They have a lot of questions and don't want to leave after discussions."

For all of these projects, Ambassador Curiel notes that the C-SPAN Archives content is unbiased with nonpartisan questions. The biggest and most obvious difference between YouTube and C-SPAN is that you get to select the clips and figure out if you want to use a 30-second point or something longer. Steve Scully used about a two-and-a-half-minute version of President Carter's "Malaise Speech" and then provided a link for students to view the whole speech. The clips reinforced what the students had read, and they were prepared to ask questions of President Carter's pollster, who was a class guest.

Each of these is an innovative class. At the heart of each is the use of the C-SPAN Video Library and the C-SPAN programming to supplement the class material. Students are exposed to the Video Library and required to research their own material. The C-SPAN material is used by the professors to illustrate points and by the students to buttress their arguments in their policy presentations. These are ideas that we hope can be emulated by others.

CHAPTER **13**

DESIGNING AND TEACHING MULTIDISCIPLINARY PROJECT-BASED TEAMS USING THE C-SPAN ARCHIVES

William Oakes, Purdue University
Carla Zoltowski, Purdue University
Patrice M. Buzzanell, Purdue University

Engineering Projects in Community Service (EPICS) began at Purdue University in 1995 with a handful of teams and a vision for multidisciplinary project-based teams working on behalf of local not-for-profits in a vertically integrated service-learning design (see https://engineering.purdue.edu/EPICS). What this means is that EPICS was developed to meet the real needs of community organizations that lack budgets and expertise to design and implement technical solutions for issues that they face. From the very beginning, EPICS involved different disciplines from across campus, worked with community partners, and involved students in their first through senior years at the university.

These main characteristics of EPICS have continued even though we have expanded considerably and now approach our 20th year anniversary. Currently we have about 400 students, in 70 different majors, registered for 31 divisions (or teams), and with a return of about 250 students in the spring semester. We have expanded from Purdue University to other university settings and to EPICS High, in which we offer design experiences at the high school level. We also have expanded from local community engagement to national and global design experiences for students (see https://engineering.purdue.edu/EPICS/Projects/Teams). For instance, our local community engagement teams have worked with local museums, schools, neighborhoods, and clinics for speech and language services. Carla Zoltowski has initiated and advised the Camp Riley (CR) team, whose description provides context and goals:

> Camp Riley is a summer camp for children with disabilities held at Bradford Woods, Indiana University's 2,500-acre universally accessible outdoor recreational facility in Martinsville, Indiana. Although the camp is very accessible, there are still barriers for the children to be able to participate fully in all of the activities. This EPICS course will focus on designing ways to overcome some of these barriers. (EPICS/Purdue, n.d.)

In expanding nationally, we joined with the Habitat for Humanity in 1996 to "lead the way in sustainable, environmentally friendly, and energy efficient practices and designing universal house plans for natural disaster relief efforts around the world" (EPICS/Purdue, 2014). Patrice has been advisor/instructor for four EPICS design teams, with the most recent being the Transforming Lives, Building Global Communities (TLBGC) team that partners with the National Society of Black Engineers (NSBE), universities, and key stakeholders in Purdue's Global Engineering Design and in Ghana to design water-energy-education solutions for two rural Ghanaian villages. Whether local, national, or international, the effectiveness of EPICS is indicated by the numbers of different universities and communities to which our program has spread. Some of the university and high school teams go by the name of EPICS, but there also are many sites that have adapted our basic aims and structures for their particular educational contexts. We encourage educational groups to translate what is applicable for their purposes. Our materials are available on our website with much more information than most readers of this chapter would ever use or want!

Our effectiveness also can be measured through students' documented abilities to operate effectively in multidisciplinary team environments, to think about design in complicated and nuanced ways, and to transition easily to workplace and virtual design experiences. Our surveys of alumni indicate that their service-learning projects prepared them for their lives outside of school. We also found that although our EPICS alums had not believed us when we told them that EPICS would prepare them for all kinds of leadership, teamwork, and design experiences in their employment and in other life contexts, they acknowledge that it did.

Now that we have provided a very brief overview, we continue with the rest of our chapter by discussing how we develop partnerships, our criteria for inclusion of projects into EPICS, and our C-SPAN team. We conclude with possibilities for future C-SPAN archival use.

EPICS PARTNERSHIPS AND THE C-SPAN ARCHIVES

In this section, we talk about partnership building and goals in EPICS before using the EPICS C-SPAN Archives team as a case that enables us to bring these points together.

EPICS Partnership Building and Goals

Because we want to provide opportunities to students for longer-term design experiences, we develop partnerships with local, national, and/or international community organizations. The traditional focus in engineering is that design is technical. More recently, however, engineering has begun to embrace human-centered design (HCD). HCD means that design processes are social, complex in social-technical intersections, and grounded in the material conditions and lived experiences of people's lives. EPICS uses HCD to capture this focus on individuals and other design stakeholders in context as well as students' needs to understand how potential design "users" might relate to and be involved in the technical solutions being developed. More than reinforcing disciplinary learning, we emphasize the need for multiple disciplinary entrée points into community projects and associated areas of impact—environmental sustainability, adaptive devices for children and adults with disabilities, use of different kinds of media to enhance educational experiences, and other areas.

There is a wealth of opportunities for projects. To integrate some of these opportunities into EPICS, we go out and meet people in the community. When we pick up projects, we discuss the project and timelines, look for project partners who are interested in working with and educating our students—not simply people who want to get a project done—and consider whether there is an optimal mix of expertise and interest available on campus, including faculty commitment to the project for several semesters. Then we start to document our ideas. The initial project description usually goes through several rounds of revision. After the project description is revised and agreed upon, the other pieces—people, equipment, space, and other project-team aspects—are pulled together. But the initial spark, the initial project description and enthusiastic community partner–EPICS expertise mix, is what ensures that an EPICS project has the potential to spawn a viable team. Put differently, our projects focus on, for example, what people wish their schools or museums had, what individuals imagine would help them navigate everyday life more easily, what communities envision would assist them in developing and sustaining a better quality of life—and what generates enthusiastic responses from students and faculty.

EPICS C-SPAN Archives Team

A confluence of factors came together several years ago when we first broached the topic of a C-SPAN Archives team in EPICS that would bridge engineering and liberal arts. The idea for the team came up in conversation when the numbers of students in EPICS were growing and we were looking to develop teams with innovative potential that could be leveraged for new partnerships. Publicity had drawn attention to the C-SPAN Archives, which was physically located on the Purdue campus at that time. The original EPICS directors, Leah Jamieson and Ed Coyle, initiated discussions with the College of Liberal Arts, particularly Robert Browning, who was not only a professor in political science but also the director of the C-SPAN Archives. The following were the main questions asked: What can we do? How could we make a project centered on the C-SPAN Archives a local community effort? (At that time, the EPICS mission centered on local agencies and not-for-profits.) How do we ensure that we maintain an appropriate scope for student team members? What realistically could students do that would combine the technical and the social?

When we considered the C-SPAN Archives, we thought that placing students in the actual archives did not make sense since the Archives itself was a large-scale national project requiring highly specialized expertise. So the original problem solving for this team was centered on determining the right scope for students. In other words, what could students realistically do in a design team that was situated locally and that was built around the C-SPAN Archives?

Another important component in these early discussions about the project team was whether we had the key personnel and multidisciplinary buy-in to move forward. On the technical side, Professor Ed Delp had the right mix of characteristics for three reasons. Ed is an electrical engineer who works with digital imagery and image recognition. He had already worked with another EPICS team to archive materials for the local historical society. Ed also had a research relationship for many years with C-SPAN in that C-SPAN funded several projects in his laboratory at Purdue. And finally, not only was he experienced with the ways things were done in EPICS, but he also had been the most successful advisor to date in integrating liberal arts students, particular history students, into a team. He explicitly valued multidisciplinary contribution. For the EPICS C-SPAN team, Ed's technical abilities in archiving, categorizing, and retrieving static and video images, plus his prior EPICS work, made him an ideal candidate for the faculty advisor role.

With these pieces in place, we took our engineering outcomes and brought them to liberal arts. The liberal arts folks thought that the course outcomes for EPICS were great for engineering, but they noted that the outcomes themselves needed be revised for different disciplinary outcomes. They helped revise the outcomes so that they reflected what would be valued and consistent with their emphases in the College of Liberal Arts and across campus. We revised to make sure that documents, goals, and course milestones were appropriate for social scientific and humanistic disciplines, particularly political science and history. We created this infrastructure over time and a little bit by accident.

During all this early development, we continued conversations about the scope and identified local governmental meetings as the site. We drafted a project description in which the initial team was tasked with creating a Lafayette archive, wondering if we could make some of our local government meetings available. After revision of the project description, the EPICS C-SPAN team was designed officially to "provide searchable meeting minutes and video for community service, containing local government and community agency meetings." Similar to the C-SPAN Archives, the aim was to help the community have free access to local government meetings. The early team members also worked with technical design elements, creating databases, Web interfaces, accessibility mechanisms, and actual recordings. They went through the processes of identifying which meetings to record, how to record meetings, and so on. Fortunately some meetings were recorded already, but others were not. In the cases where there were not video records, the students had to make recordings themselves.

This team began in spring 2005 and ended in 2010. The idea worked—archives of local government meetings were recorded, categorized, and made available to others. Moreover, students gained experience in the technical design work as well as an understanding of the archives' importance. However, over time we struggled with a few points. For instance, there was a lot of early design work in developing the structure for the local archive. The initial coding was done by the early teams that established the structure for the archival work. At the point when the team was mostly doing recording rather than design, it became less interesting to the technical students. Questions arose about sustainability and whether the mission of this team to create greater access to and interest in local government was fulfilled. After discussions about interest in maintaining the team and after reviewing some recent reorganizing of software teams within EPICS, the different stakeholders decided to end this particular team but felt that the project had been successful.

POSSIBILITIES FOR FUTURE C-SPAN ARCHIVAL USE

As we reflect upon possibilities for future design teams using the C-SPAN Archives or a modification of the archive concept on the local level, we keep in mind the overall strength of design and multidisciplinary projects in academe. Our mindset is that we want to create real world experiences that prepare students for a future of collaboration, teamwork, and learning through iterative phases of problem setting and problem solving. In a traditional university class, the assumption is that students come in and do not know much or anything about the topic. After 15 weeks or so if they are operating within a semester system, the students are supposed to know everything about a subject. If you have a class project, it begins and ends with the class. Everything magically aligns. But when you are doing things like recording school board meetings and these recordings are not fully digitized by the end of the semester, well, what do you do? Our structure in EPICS is such that students can continue with projects over two or more semesters. Indeed, some of our students stay in EPICS for their entire undergraduate experience. This notion of design processes that span semesters and develop sustainable solutions for particular communities coincides with engagement models in which we as instructors believe that students can do something that will have short- and long-term impacts, and that we advise or facilitate the process. We are breaking the traditional academic mindset. In doing so, we are integrating a number of processes into the curriculum. These processes include innovation, problem solving, design, analysis, resourcefulness, disciplinary fundamentals, ethics, science, teamwork, mathematics, and communication. EPICS and similar project-based learning experiences have the potential to realize new efficiencies in the curriculum.

We have been talking about Purdue University but, as mentioned earlier, we work with a number of different universities and high schools. We thrive on long-term partnerships. We have taken our model to different places and have seen it adapted for different purposes.

We believe that the C-SPAN Archives case offers new possibilities. The push for science, technology, engineering, and math (STEM) disciplinary knowledge to meet national and global challenges is not going to work unless such knowledge is integrated into other disciplines and the benefits of these non-STEM disciplines is recognized as vital to design success. If we return to the C-SPAN Archives example, the EPICS team integrated technology, government, political science, communication, public relations for publicity, local community partnerships, and so on. We could envision middle and high schools taking our basic model and integrating the C-SPAN Archives and a local government archive into government, American history, and other classes. We already have examples of ways to integrate the C-SPAN video clips into mass communication and political science classes, but we maintain that the technical and social aspects could be bridged easily if high school combinations of computing and government, for instance, take place. There is enormous potential for these kinds of hybrid and project-based classes. They cross disciplinary areas and use current database tools with some design work to create new local archives in varied areas of interest. We also encourage use of our model to build multidisciplinary team interactions into learning communities.

In developing service-learning projects, we encourage students to appreciate the fact that they do not have the sole disciplinary expertise to solve today's challenges. We encourage them to learn how to interact with team members and project partners who come from diverse backgrounds. We want them to understand how they can make the world a better place during their college years and later when they are in a career path where they can have engaged professions.

PART V

FUTURE POSSIBILITIES

CHAPTER **14**

PARTISANSHIP WITHOUT ALTERNATIVES: KEYNOTE REFLECTIONS ON C-SPAN AND MY MOTHER[1]

Roderick P. Hart, University of Texas at Austin

Whenever I think of C-SPAN, I think of my mother. She was a C-SPAN junkie. She loved the interviews; she loved the historical accounts; but, mostly, she loved the partisanship. "I love it when they fight," she often said. She loved the Sturm und Drang of politics until the day she died. And she died, almost predictably, on the most political day of the year—July 4th—the same day of the year that Thomas Jefferson and John Adams died. My mother was the most political of the three.

Her story is not exceptional but it is familiar. Her Irish immigrant father was killed in a horse and buggy accident in Connecticut prior to her birth; she graduated from Pawtucket High School in Rhode Island (where she was the class poet) and then married my father, the eldest of 9, who himself had become head of his mother's household at age 18. Neither of my parents went to college, and yet their 4 children amassed 10 college degrees among them. An American story, this.

A mother becomes a different mother for each of her children. For my older sister, Mom was a member of the Altar Society and the Women's Sodality; for my younger sister she was a consummate wit, a jokester; for my brother she was an aficionado of all things Irish; for me she was a political animal.

Unsurprisingly, she choreographed my first political experience. The year was 1952 and the place, Somerset, Massachusetts. Dwight Eisenhower was to pass by my house in a grand cavalcade. I purloined my mother's broom handle and a piece of cardboard, made an "I Like Ike" sign, and stationed myself among the neighbors who had gathered on our lawn. A shadow quickly loomed over me, the sign and broom handle snatched from my hand. The face was stern, the sentence abrupt: "Not in this house."

This is my first political memory. Mom and I never spoke of the incident again, but I still remember her odd sentence (it had no subject, it had no verb). I also remember the emotion in her voice. It would be years before I would learn what it meant to be born Irish Catholic at the turn of the century in a nation not yet pleased with its growing diversity. My mother taught me, pellucidly, what it meant to be a Democrat or a Republican.

Politics came with the sunrise for her—first the *Today* show, then the morning newspaper. Her midday angelus was C-SPAN; dinnertime brought her Dan Rather. In the evening she sought out *Firing Line* and she went to sleep listening to talk radio.

A dutiful son, I phoned home regularly. The ritual never varied: my life, my wife's life, the grandchildren, two risqué jokes, and then politics: "You won't believe what this mayor of ours is up to." "What's wrong with that governor of yours?" "Sis is out campaigning for the town selectman." "Have you heard the new Hillary joke?" If you were Mary Claire Sullivan Hart's child and had no interest in politics, life would have been difficult for you.

Politics was my mother's compass; it helped her navigate her world. She never forgot she was an American citizen and she never forgot the old discriminations. My father was a child of the future ("Don't look back" was his motto) but my mother mentored the past ("Never forget your own kind," she often declared).

Partisan though she was, she never stopped learning. The day before her stroke she watched politics on television and, more important, she had an *attitude* about what she watched.

My mother's story is an old story and that's a shame. Today, with the economy erratic and with politicians in disarray, it is easy to abandon the commonweal. But my mother knew that ceding power to others is just plain dumb and, worse, self-compromising. When my mother died on July 4, 2000, the United States lost a voter. We need a replacement. We need several.

But politics is having a hard time, and that's what I want to discuss in this chapter. To my mother's way of thinking, C-SPAN is a glorious thing. It brings us politics raw, politics unvarnished; but people have lost a taste for politics. They hate it when politicians mix it up, when they decry one another's policy preferences. They want politics without tears.

My mother knew that that was nonsense. She knew that contested ideas and deeply felt passions lie at the very heart of politics. She knew that the whole point of democracy is to pit the forces of good and evil against one another and then decide which is which. She knew that most political parties are born out of resentment—resentment about other classes, other regions, other ethnicities, other interest groups, other age cohorts. And when you put all of these contestants on the field at the same time, as C-SPAN does, you get the United States of America at its best.

So say I. Others disagree, and I'd like to talk about them today. I want to talk about the C-SPAN avoiders, those desiring an antiseptic politics, politics without its affirmative passions. These gainsayers come in two varieties: (1) Web Evangelists and (2) Uncivil Louts. The former finds hope in political interactions based on new technologies; they want to make politics a mental thing rather than an existential thing. They are idealists, these Evangelists, and they believe that the World Wide Web and a plethora of mobile devices will tidy up politics.

The Uncivil Louts are cut from a different cloth. They decry politicians' self-interestedness and, really, all forms of political give-and-take. They yearn for a day when the pettiness of politics will be transcended, but they only imagine that for a moment or two. At all other times, they abandon the very concept of political accommodation.

The Web Evangelists and the Uncivil Louts are perfectly suited to the modern age. They capture a zeitgeist fashioned out of deferral. My mother would have found that abhorrent. While she was fascinated by the Web and while she loved political humor, she knew that politics was a knock-down, drag-out affair on its best days and that that was its glory. She knew that contestation—full-bodied, take-no-prisoners contestation—is what purifies ideas and makes them socially palatable. C-SPAN tells this story each day, thereby honoring the political enterprise. Others, however, tell a different tale.

THE WEB EVANGELISTS

As someone who has spent a good deal of his professional career doing computerized content analysis, I am no Luddite. Indeed, I am attracted to any modality that would make people smarter about politics or make them feel more passionate about voting. So I find the questions posed by the cybernetic age truly profound: Is genuine deliberation possible via Internet modalities? Does the Web focus us on public policies or political personalities? Has the Internet increased social fragmentation by decentralizing information sources? Are the new media abetting Americans' civic disengagement? Are smartphones, smart mobs, and always-on connections changing democracy as we know it?

Generally speaking, though, I am not sanguine about the civic possibilities of new media for this reason: A democracy depends on persons of known identity interacting with others of the same sort. You will immediately see my problem: the Internet masks identity and it does so aggressively, athletically. Each day, the Internet invites us to revel in our anonymity, to become scions of voyeurism. A democracy, in contrast, requires transparency of identity. A democracy depends on ideas, of course, but it mostly depends on people to body forth those ideas. A democracy depends on interactions among those whose motives can be weighed and judged, people who *stand with* the positions they take.

The Internet demands no such thing. It entices us with a sea of pseudonyms, letting us match our multiple e-mail addresses with our multiple personalities. For these reasons, pornography has become the Internet's stock-in-trade. Across the nation, across the world, unknown persons download images of other unknown persons for autoerotic pleasure. No relationships here. No intercourse either. Just isolated individuals doing what comes electronically. A torrent of images, an avalanche of orgasms. All by yourself.

I have a good friend who is a successful lobbyist in Austin. To you he may seem eccentric for he does not use e-mail, never mind Twitter. In fact, he doesn't write things down at all. He reasons that words prematurely printed can undermine deals not yet fully fashioned. And so he uses his prodigious memory and a surgically implanted cell phone to do his business. More important, he uses *his body* to do his business. He slaps people's backs to signal camaraderie, searches their eyes to spot a potential agreement, shakes their hands to confirm a bargain. Lobbyists, that is, press the flesh. When feeling prurient, they don't go to the Internet; they go to strip clubs—because that's where the bodies are.

I truly do not understand why one would listen to those whose identities they cannot confirm. Sure, subscription e-mails are useful. They tell us where the conference will be held and how the convention hotel can be contacted. And, sure, social media are fun, allowing us to make black marks on our computer screens while others make black marks on their computer screens in response. There's a lot of loneliness out there and, if the Internet can reduce that, it does no harm. But there is no loneliness in politics, for politics is the business of communities. It *requires* exposure.

The issues being discussed in this volume are important to me as one professionally concerned with declining levels of civic engagement in the United States.[2] Because of these unhappy trends, I am ready to embrace any technology that will extricate our fellow citizens from their recliners and thrust them back into the public sphere. I am especially concerned that today's young people—the avatars of the new technologies—are abandoning traditional politics for the virtualities of their age. I do not know if the Internet can bring them back into the fold but, if it can, I am all for it.

But I do not believe it will. As a medium, the Internet delivers personality and emotion poorly, and personality and emotion are the very essence of political persuasion. Citizens, after all, usually grope their way to the polling place, relying on their vague intuitions about public character and their often poorly supported but very human impressions about whom to trust and why. I'm not sure that computers can change these habits. I'm not sure that they should.

One hears a great deal these days about virtual communities. Communities? I'm not so sure. Real communities, I submit, are economic or ethnic or geographic or demographic or religious in nature. Real communities are mobilized organically, not artificially. Real communities observe civic and cultural rituals together—they paint the neighborhood school when the city's coffers run low; raise money for the Scouts and cut the grass for the Little League team. Real communities have a sense of place, a sense of contiguity. Members of these communities often do not know one another's names but they know one another's faces. Given the importance of communities and the distancing effects of the Internet, I put this question to the reader: Do you feel good about trusting the future of this nation to a gaggle of lonely typists?

Politically speaking, the Internet performs best when it delivers timely and comprehensive information, surely an important commodity in civic life. The Internet also delivers political ideology, and that is its glory when it is not its embarrassment. Information and ideology are central to an engaged democracy, but can they sustain it? According to some, yes. Anecdotal reports suggest that the Internet helps activist groups mobilize and political parties garner campaign contributions. Too, innovators continue to launch interesting political experiments. Doug Bailey's Freedom Channel, Tracy Westen's Democracy Network, and the Markle Foundation's Web White and Blue project are interesting adjuncts to traditional forms of engagement.

But Internet politics is cerebral politics, sitting-down politics, and we already have enough of both. What we need is more standing-up politics, more get-out-of-the-house politics. A vital democracy needs critics to keep it honest, but it needs activists to thrive. And so a New Age question continues to bother me: Can the e-person become a citizen? I'm not sure. As I see the members of the e-generation, they stress information over affect, speed over deliberation, individualism over community, and libertarianism over representativeness. Political trust comes hard to this generation. Even as its members surround themselves with information, it is hard to get their attention.

The e-generation thinks of government as an oaf, as a too-large, un-nimble giant that always gets things wrong. With the Web at their fingertips, e-pioneers can sail past the obdurate problems of crime, hunger, and disease and find a cyber-pal somewhere in the vast beyond. But even as they and their pal sail past, government stumbles along, doing its best to educate children, patrol highways, stop drug abuse, and care for the elderly simply because that is what a decent society does. Problems like these call for slow, expensive, collaborative work and they do not yield to a computer fix (as the Affordable Care Act initially reminded us). These are problems that make people emotional and that sometimes tear communities apart. These are problems lying at the very center of politics. They do not lie in cyberspace.

Or so say I. At this point in history, we only have opinions to guide us since so little hard evidence has been collected about digital democracy. What little evidence we do have shows that more and more people are online these days and that political information has become fairly easy to locate. But once political information is located, I ask, what will we *do* with it? There is a digital divide, yes, but there is also an affect divide and it is that divide that worries me most. Somehow, we must remind ourselves that a society without government is ungovernable and that a society without politics is unpalatable. To forget that premise is to forget the very nature of politics, and that sort of forgetting would surely be the death of us all.

THE UNCIVIL LOUTS

Even before the shooting of Congresswoman Gabrielle Giffords several years ago, political incivility had been in the news. The Tea Party had been ranting and raving, a sitting member of Congress had heckled the president during a speech to Congress, a storied civil rights leader had been subjected to the N-word 40 years after that historic legislation was passed, a Cuban American TV personality had used ethnic innuendos to expose a Jewish American's ethnic innuendos, bloggers of all stripes had been running amok, and a popular cable personality had attacked a liberal academic who was then subjected to death threats.[3]

Commentators have wrung their hands about such matters, claiming that political incivility has reached new heights in the United States. They have argued further that incivility is sidelining voters, causing them to abandon political engagement. What produces these waves of incivility? Some have traced them to major political transitions (e.g., when one long-standing establishment is replaced by another), to changing demographic trends and the cultural sensibilities they usher in, and to especially feverish times as, for example, when a nation is attacked (viz 9/11) or when the economy slackens. Other explanations also exist: political parties become polarized, term-limited politicians see no need to befriend their colleagues, politics becomes more professionalized and hence more anomic, and the mass media become dominant, encouraging a coarseness of expression not found in face-to-face cultures (American Enterprise Institute for Public Policy Research, 2007).

Political incivility may be depraved but it is also popular. Talk radio has become famous for its invectiveness, while cable "news" shows further spread the outrage. Too, as the political pie is sliced thinner and thinner, and as activist cadres become increasingly removed from the political center, they increasingly feel entitled to let loose. In addition, schoolyard bullying is on the rise. Might this be children's ways of acting out the polarities their parents find so compelling?

In light of these trends, commentators have proposed a bevy of solutions: (1) recruit a new breed of leaders worthy of being emulated rather than disparaged; (2) send our most rapacious politicians to civility school to brush up on their manners; (3) censor news personnel who goad politicians into taking cheap shots at one another; (4) send the electorate to church to reduce their blood lust. For many observers, political incivility is a known evil and its remedies lie at hand.

I disagree. I believe that political incivility is an exceedingly complex matter and that its cures are not at all apparent. I also believe that the whole issue of political incivility has been approached backwardly. We have too often assumed that incivility is obviously unattractive, but I find its attractiveness to be its bulwark against eradication. Until we reckon squarely with why people are uncivil to one another and why bystanders secretly enjoy such interchanges, we cannot upend it. In contrast to commentators on the Left, I believe that incivility is usually *not* a sign of an engaged and robust democracy but quite the opposite: a sign of wanton self-regard and an abandonment of the skills needed to make politics functional.

Space is not sufficient to make this latter case, but I do want to ask why incivility is lovable. *Lovable?* My reasoning is that only that which is loved can survive. Families are loved; families survive. Music is loved; music survives. Football is loved; football survives. But much else survives as well: war, poverty, envy, acquisitiveness. All endure because they are loved. Kenneth Burke (1969, p. 22) tells us that war is the "ultimate disease of cooperation" whereby two adversaries agree to engage one another at a particular time, at a particular place, over particular matters. Should these agreements cease, should war become unlovable, wars would end. So, too, with poverty. Somebody, somebodies, reason that fixing the problem—via massive redistribution of wealth, or even modest redistribution of wealth—is less attractive than eliminating poverty in a fortnight, as could surely be done. Poverty persists, poverty is loved, because its remedies are judged more reprehensible.

Political incivility presents similar circumstances. It waxes and wanes from era to era, but in the United States it has been a hardy perennial. In that sense it is like crabgrass. There is something in nature that also loves crabgrass and so it flourishes despite our best efforts, or our nominal efforts. We could eliminate crabgrass in an instant by paving over our front yards but that would be seen as too expensive, or aesthetically displeasing, or environmentally problematic, and so crabgrass persists, loved for its own self, loved more than its alternatives. But why would anyone love incivility? I sketch out eight reasons here.

1. *Because it is dramatic.* Incivility crops up when people are anxious, when they lose control, when their feelings override their cerebration. Inevitably, that which is out of control attracts our attention. The Indianapolis 500, for example, is almost constantly out of control (a significant number of persons have been killed since the race began in 1911) and yet it attracts 400,000 spectators each year. Who can turn away when death stalks the Brickyard? Similarly, who can turn away when Sean Hannity sallies forth? And unlike the 500, incivility is always about something important—justice, freedom, life-and-death—and so we inevitably return its gaze.

2. *Because it is dialectical.* Incivility is Janus-like. It looks fore and aft simultaneously; its denunciations are inspired by someone else's affirmations. Social life, of course, is never two-sided. Like the physical world, it is bewilderingly multidimensional. Public policy decisions inevitably inspire a thousand options. But who could cope with so many alternatives? And so we board the Arc of Politics two-by-two: Democrats vs. Republicans, isolationists vs.

internationalists, free-spenders vs. penny-pinchers. All of them stride the deck and shout at one another. Who could stop their ears to such a din?

3. *Because it is personified.* It is not surprising that television has become a haven for incivility. There, policy issues take on palpably human form. Keith Olbermann becomes the instantiation of smarmy liberalism, Newt Gingrich of smarmy conservatism. We adore such characters and revile them. We read about them in *Time* but also in *People* magazine. We get to know their human frailties, their families, their saintliness and adulteries. As a result, when the snarkiness commences, it becomes easier to choose sides, to become "identified" with such persons and, hence, with the causes they embody.

4. *Because it is gentrified.* Incivility stops short of engaging our basest passions. It has an intellectual patina to it; it comingles ideas and feelings. Incivility is violence arrested, hatred gone middle-class. Possessed as it is of such qualities, incivility even resists its own naming. You call me uncivil; I call myself deeply committed. I call you uncivil; you call yourself a patriot. Others decry us both as uncivil; we describe ourselves as truth tellers. "If you can't stand the heat get out of the kitchen" goes the verse. "Politics is not pattycakes" goes the refrain. Culinarily, incivility is kimchi for the political class.

5. *Because it is expulsive.* Politics exists because of original sin. Had Eve not tempted Adam so beguilingly, we'd have no need for it. By now, however, the wages of their sins have become manifest: Nothing works very well. Territories are hard to share; skin color separates us; tribes won't cooperate; good ideas die aborning; things cost too much; people are prickly. It's enough to make grown men cry. And so they do—each night on Fox; each day in the city square. Incivility is as primal as primates can get in a modern age. Incivility has its roots in what makes us human: our differences.

6. *Because it is compensatory.* Life's tragedies spring from the contingencies we face. We inherit the present from the past and hence are constrained (e.g., the national debt). The future is not yet here and so we must plan things tentatively (e.g., social security reform). As J. L. Austin and colleagues (1962) might say, incivility is performative, a way of accomplishing something when nothing else can be done—right now, put in place forever. Engaging our passions, crying into the night, thus feels like a *doing*. What else could explain the sense of camaraderie and accomplishment some people feel when Ted Cruz lashes out?

7. *Because it is poetic.* Incivility has a kind of pedestrian beauty. It appeals both to the eye (via metaphor) and the ear (via antithesis). "Romance is rape embellished with meaningful looks" declare the feminists (Cummins & Bindel, 2007).[4] Hurricane Katrina "cleaned up public housing in New Orleans" respond the conservatives (Sasser, 2006). One commentator (Martin, 2010) says the Confederates "were, and forever will be, domestic terrorists," to which another responds: "Islamic terrorists don't hate America like liberals do. . . . If they had that much energy, they'd have indoor plumbing by now." When happening upon incivility we find language at play. One could resist its charms, but why?

8. *Because it is commemorative.* Politics continues, seemingly forever. A bill that dies on the floor of Congress finds new life a month later. Via politics, old wars can be fought again and old prejudices never forgotten. Uncivil discourse exploits the wounds that will not heal, constantly calling to mind the indignities of the past. With incivility at one's side, one can never lose . . . forever. Instead, one can resurrect the past—for example, the Reagan years—lionizing the Gipper as the seer who undid the Soviet Union or denouncing him as the wastrel who accelerated the national debt. With incivility, destiny rides to the fray yet again.

Incivility is not one thing; it is many things. It may seem perverse to focus on its attractions as I have done here, but incivility cannot be defeated until we reckon with its seductions. The most obvious alternative to incivility, of course, is to find something else to do with our time. Incivility is poetic but not very good poetry, so one might instead read some Keats. Incivility is commemorative but its memories are horribly inaccurate, so one might read some Stephen Ambrose as well. There is nothing inherently wrong with the desires mentioned above, but one need not call Barack Obama a Muslim socialist to satisfy them. Indeed, dancing with Ellen Degeneres meets most of these needs and improves cardiovascular fitness as well.

Yes, dancing is silly and politics important. Too important, I argue, for thoughtlessness. No doubt, uncivil discourse has its place—when grievances abound and when avenues for addressing them have been explored and found wanting. But that is gold-plated incivility, the stuff of great revolutions. The kinds of incivility that bother me are the banal sorts, those coarse and unthinking responses to the irritations of everyday life. Especially irksome are those who *market* incivility to the masses: Rush Limbaugh, shock-news stations, Howard Stern, gangsta rap, Jon Stewart, Neal Boortz. It is one thing to be uncivil and quite another to export it at a profit.

Above all, incivility must not become fodder for everyday human commerce. We can avoid it with only the slightest effort. Incivility is a boorish indulgence, language divorced from grand purpose. It exacerbates the cross-cutting cleavages already inherent in politics and it is dehumanizing and uncreative as well. It feels good to be uncivil and it televises well, but we humans are meant for bigger things. A serious people, a caring people, an enlightened people, can do better.

CONCLUSION

That, of course, brings us back to C-SPAN, whose archives cry out for more scholarly research but which also stand for the centrality of politics in democratic life. C-SPAN'S founder, Brian Lamb, is a visionary who reverences public dialogue. No doubt he uses the Internet to get information but he also understands that the Web is a simulacrum, a device for hovering above politics but not for *being* political. *Being* political requires beings—human ones—who enter the lists replete with names, faces, bodies, and voices. Real politics, everyday politics, important politics is a blood sport because it deals with crucial human issues instead of deferring them.

On their best days, politicians do such work civilly, as they should. Indeed, if one had the patience to collect all the instances of incivility committed during the last year in the United States, I doubt one would find much of it on C-SPAN. Despite their legion imperfections, that is, politicians themselves know how to be civil. They bellow and holler and call each other names from time to time but only occasionally. Perhaps that claim seems odd. Perhaps the reader will point to the evening rants on Fox and MSNBC as counterexamples. But only a dozen or so members of Congress are seen on such shows and they are usually chosen because they behave badly on cue. As they are doing so, however, the other 523 members of Congress are back on Capitol Hill trying to strike a deal.

I try not to be a Pollyanna about politics but I rarely succeed. I have endless admiration for the people who make our laws because I, for one, do not know how much health care should cost or when, or if, we should send troops to Syria. Problems like these are enormously complex and rarely admit to simple solutions. All of us who care about democracy should debate these issues, but we've got our own lives to live and so we hire out such work to those who make our laws. They, in turn, do the best they can, deprived of omniscience as they are and hampered, too, by ego and ambition.

Each day, C-SPAN tells us this story of politics and personality. How lucky we are that it does. My mother knew the glories of C-SPAN and she respected it profoundly. So do I. So should we all.

NOTES

1. Portions of this chapter came to life in lectures delivered over the course of several years at the University of Virginia, George Washington University, Texas A&M University, and Louisiana State University. I am indebted to the faculty and students at those institutions for their interest in these matters and for their feedback.

2. The author is the founding director of the Annette Strauss Institute at the University of Texas at Austin. For additional information see http://moody.utexas.edu/strauss.

3. The cast of characters mentioned here include Rep. Joe Wilson (R-SC), Rep. John Lewis (D-GA), CNN's Rick Sanchez, Comedy Central's Jon Stewart, the Fox Network's Glenn Beck, and C.U.N.Y.'s Frances Fox Piven.

4. A quotation popularly attributed to Andrea Dworkin.

CHAPTER **15**

REFLECTIONS ON THE POTENTIAL AND CHALLENGES OF THE C-SPAN ARCHIVES FOR DISCOVERY, LEARNING, AND ENGAGEMENT

Patrice M. Buzzanell, Purdue University

In rereading sections, particularly the opening remarks, of the earlier chapters of this book in preparation for this final chapter, I discovered a few things that I believe are the heart of this book. The first is that all of the chapter authors are clearly passionate about their topics and about their unique uses of the C-SPAN Archives. Their passion is expressed through the engaging way they present their stories and data excerpts. Another aspect is their candor about the context of their work and how they situate themselves vis-à-vis their discovery and learning experiences. Finally, the authors implicitly if not explicitly encourage engagement with different communities. In other words, the chapter authors share their work because they are interested in prompting conversation about the real challenges that we all face in today's world by delving deeply into the past for the unvarnished and unedited excerpts of everyday life provided by the C-SPAN Archives and by pulling forward agendas that can enable readers to become the experts, to do the archival research, and to participate in informed discussion that can assist communities and, indeed, our nation and the world. They clearly have expertise but present themselves more so as co-learners and engaged citizens eager to highlight their own contributions to ongoing conversations in their areas than experts who have all the answers.

These aspects—passion, unique entrée points into the C-SPAN Archives, candor, and engagement—are evident from the very first pages of this collection. Readers can see these characteristics in Brian Lamb's penchant for telling very vivid stories that provide insight into C-SPAN's history, mission, and design. As he lays out C-SPAN's relatively modest beginnings and its champions, I believe that readers will feel as I did, that we were and are there both sharing in the history of this unique enterprise and also contemplating with Brian its uncertain future in terms of funding and technologies. As Brian so aptly describes the current phase in C-SPAN: "C-SPAN is sitting in the middle off all this dynamic change in the industry, holding on for dear life." With this edited volume, readers probably feel as though they, too, are going along for the ride but, more importantly, are envisioning how they, and the chapter authors, can and do contribute to making the C-SPAN Archives an even more vital aspect of everyday life.

The commitment of key people in developing and sustaining C-SPAN comes across in Brian Lamb's candid remarks, and is reinforced by Robert Browning's explanation of the technologies involved in the C-SPAN Archives and the evolving development of its indexing, clipping, and other capabilities. Finally, building on Susan Swain's remarks about her enthusiasm for this book, I too hope that these essays will encourage the academic community to embrace the affordances of the online Video Library (http://www.c-span.org) and develop its uses in innovative and far-reaching ways.

This edited collection demonstrates explicitly that in capturing, archiving, and closed captioning congressional hearings as well as live interview/call-in programs and coverage of U.S. Senate debates without editing or editorial comment, not only does the C-SPAN Archives offer snapshots in time about political thinking and practices but also that the Archives continues to expand in content and format (e.g., nonfiction books and historical programs). The chapter authors offer their insights into how they and others might reflect upon and implement different uses for the C-SPAN Archives in discovery, learning, and engagement.

Furthermore, this collection can serve to encourage archivists and librarians working with media collections to look to the C-SPAN Archives for inspiration into how their collections could be similarly utilized. This latter use is especially important because librarians are called upon to support information resource needs for faculty, particularly the increasing demand for video as raw material for teaching and research. Moreover, interdisciplinary scholars working in U.S. and global politics and policy would find this edited collection useful for explicating arguments depicted in the C-SPAN Archives for funding and other purposes. As a result, this source book operates ahead of the curve in terms of increased demand for video in academe for many different reasons.

REFLECTIONS ON CHAPTER CONTRIBUTIONS

As a preview to the commentary in this section, I first (a) provide the prompts to authors for writing their chapters and then (b) discuss their contributions to discovery, learning, and engagement.

First, by providing a set of questions, each of the chapter authors was encouraged to produce an essay that would lend coherence to the entire collection despite differences among these authors' disciplinary foci, theoretical and/or methodological bases, and contexts. The goal was to achieve some consistencies in chapter structures without discouraging creative expansions of these guidelines. For those chapters that focus on scholarship and engagement opportunities using the C-SPAN Archives—namely, those in the "Research Case Studies" area (Parts II and III of this volume)—authors were asked to reflect upon the following questions:

- What do the C-SPAN Archives contribute (e.g., what added value to the research project does the Archives present)?
- How might the video be used (i.e., what type of video, analysis of the video, findings, especially what the C-SPAN video contributes theoretically and pragmatically to particular content areas)?

- What do you consider to be future directions of research and engagement based on your chapter?

The goal of these research guidelines was to find out from chapter authors what might be of interest to the broad audience anticipated for this book but also what theoretical and pragmatic contributions and implications might be derived from and spur further use of the C-SPAN Archives.

For those chapters that focus on learning and engagement opportunities using the C-SPAN Archives—"Teaching Case Studies" (Part IV)—authors were asked to provide some course specifications and commentary as follows:

- What is the level and idea or concept of the course that uses the C-SPAN Archives?
- How could the C-SPAN Archives be used in this course and how would the video illustrate the concepts under discussion?
- How might the C-SPAN Archives video contribute to learning beyond non-video teaching?
- What would you recommend for future directions of C-SPAN Archives use?

Here, too, with the guiding questions the intent was to encourage authors to provide ideas about innovative uses of the C-SPAN Archives in learning contexts that also combined and fostered further discovery and learning. Because contexts differ in terms of resources allocated to teaching, curriculum, technologies, and other aspects supportive of learning goals, the hope was that these chapters would inspire creative adaptations based on local opportunities.

With these opening reflections and organizing questions in mind, I now turn to the second part of this section. Here examination of the chapters enables reflection on their different discovery, learning, and engagement emphases. As readers will have noted in the different parts of this book, these emphases often are intertwined. Following their order in this book, in this chapter I discuss the "Research Case Studies," "Teaching Case Studies," and the keynote address by Rod Hart.

Beginning with the "Research Case Studies" (Parts II and III), authors offer quite varied ways in which C-SPAN archival data can be examined and why. For most of the authors, the data are both communication data worthy of examination in their own rights (i.e., examination of communication itself as in the ongoing constitutive process of communicating) and provide the texts and socio-political-cultural understandings upon which research in communication, political science, history, consumer science, and interdisciplinary projects can be based. As a result, readers learn not simply how the data were assembled and analyzed for each author's purposes but also how others have acted upon the archived messages within the contexts in which they were uttered as well as their implications for the here and now. Examining these data from rhetorical, historical, and social scientific—both qualitative and quantitative—lenses means that the research case studies offer a number of different ways to develop scholarly projects.

For instance, in his chapter "Preserving Black Political Agency in the Age of Obama: Utilizing the C-SPAN Video Archives in Rhetorical Scholarship" (Chapter 4), Theon Hill examines rhetorics of social change, particularly the prophetic tradition, and how and why such discourse may or may not hold political figures such as President Obama accountable for their actions.

In Chapter 5, using her vantage point as historian, Kathryn Brownell looks "behind the headlines" of the 1984 election to find out what the C-SPAN archival data can tell readers about the ways individuals in local communities engaged with national politics. Here, the data are not examined for the meaning-making processes per se but as tools for use in figuring out how and why people behaved as they did at a particular point in the U.S. political landscape.

In Chapter 6, Colene Lind also follows a rhetorical tradition in scholarship but focuses on town hall meetings. Through her analysis of these public forums held by U.S. senators and representatives, she provides insight into what her analyses indicate is unprincipled leadership, effective leadership demeanors, leadership for the people that harbors a hint of defiance, and leadership-followership dynamics present not only in governmental venues but that manifest differently in all organizing activities. Rhetoric is the means by which political actors negotiate the tensions, the "delicate rhetorical dance," that can contribute to effectiveness.

Rather than focusing on the Archives as a context in which the constitutive nature of rhetoric is illuminated, as Theon Hill and Colene Lind did, in Chapter 7 Stephanie Bor examines reported uses of the Archives. Specifically, she describes how she gathered and analyzed data through qualitative content analysis of survey and interview techniques to uncover themes that guided C-SPAN employees' strategic uses of the C-SPAN Archives in the production and dissemination of news. Moving from communication emphases but consistent with his background as a consumer scientist and director of the Center for Professional Selling at Purdue University, in Chapter 8 Christopher Kowal treats the C-SPAN Video Archives as a great resource for academic/political market research. In his chapter, Christopher shifts further away from the discourse within the archival videos and from employees' perceptions about and reported uses of the Archives to delve into C-SPAN programming effects on consumer and voting behaviors as well innovative techniques being used to detect the impact of emotion on political behavior. Similarly, in Chapter 9, Sorin Matei is interested in supporting public affairs debate and data journalism, rather than an investigation of rhetoric and perceived or reported communication. In conceptualizing intersecting threads of interactive data as a "network of debate," Sorin notes that the C-SPAN records can be analyzed to locate nodes at different levels. These nodes can be at the semantic as well as the interactional or actor levels, with implications for a "social network analysis 'practice capital' approach" in which visualization indicates graphically who says what to whom in addition to how much is said. These nodes can be considered as resources for policy research and journalism.

So, what do readers learn from these research case study chapters? In reflecting upon these scholars' work, one can step back from the particular aspects of their data and analytic techniques to focus on some of the social, political, and market challenges to which they contribute. They promote greater understanding of how arguments are framed, how tensions in leadership-followership and community engagement are managed, and the meaningfulness and outcomes of the work of individuals and groups in contemporary society. Each sees the C-SPAN Archives as an underutilized resource for conceptualizing and studying certain issues. Each reveals his or her own values and those underlying the construction of the C-SPAN Archives. Each provides cultural depth into ways of living, making sense of, and interacting with others in the world. Clearly, there is much more that each of these scholars contributes. I hope that these chapters will act as a springboard for further endeavors in discovery.

Similarly, the chapters in Part IV, "Teaching Case Studies," also function as a starting point, but more so for learning rather than discovery and engagement. Key to this section—indeed the entire book—is Chapter 11, in which Robert Browning walks readers through clipping features, assignments, and other details in a hands-on way that is useful for "teaching American government concepts using C-SPAN" but also for classes in other areas of academe. These other classes could include the forums promoting high involvement by students given the instructions that Robert describes in Chapter 12, "Interactive Learning In and Out of the Classroom." In this chapter, Robert describes courses designed and implemented by the founder and executive director of the Purdue Institute for Civic Communication, Ambassador Carolyn Curiel; C-SPAN's founder, Brian Lamb; and C-SPAN's politics senior executive producer, Steve Scully, at different academic institutions and with different uses for the C-SPAN Archives.

In "Teaching Case Studies," other authors use the C-SPAN Archives for diverse purposes in communication and in engineering education. Glenn Sparks approaches his case study as both theoretical and practical in terms of his uses for the C-SPAN Archives in his mass communication course. Glenn provides an overview of three videos selected from the Archives that make specific points relevant to theories under class discussion and that are controversial in their own right. In an approach similar to Robert Browning's, Glenn provides details about specific assignments. Like other chapter authors in this section, he views the C-SPAN Archives as offering limitless possibilities for instruction.

Although not captured in chapter form for this book but aligning with Glenn Sparks's uses of the C-SPAN Archives in communication courses, the National Communication Association (NCA)—under the direction of Trevor Parry-Giles, NCA's associate director for academic and professional affairs, and the NCA headquarters office—has begun a coordinated search of the C-SPAN Video Library to create a playlist of communication scholars who have been featured and/or interviewed. This playlist is under development, with the daunting challenge of organizing and reflecting upon the very extensive collection of communication scholars featured in the Archives.

The final chapter in Part IV offers a discussion about the award-winning and funded program, Engineering Projects in Community Service (EPICS). As co-directors and/or long-term faculty members in EPICS, Bill Oakes, Carla Zoltowski, and Patrice Buzzanell present opportunities to engage middle school, high school, and college students in multidisciplinary learning and community engagement through service-learning teams. Bill, Carla, and Patrice discuss a C-SPAN Archives team that developed technological infrastructures and community inroads into local political and social issues. Although EPICS has been replicated in part and in whole in high schools and universities in the United States and beyond, these authors discuss how the ideas and website resources developed by EPICS could be used in different educational settings and for different purposes.

Just as the closing of the research case discussion in this chapter offered an opportunity to reflect upon the insights derived from examination of the scholarship, this seems like an opportune time to reflect upon the opportunities afforded by the cases in Part IV. Chapter authors' overviews of these different teaching models and of how they have incorporated the C-SPAN Archives are inspirational. Although these chapters are not long, the authors provide details about specific assignments, student responses and questions, and some changes in policies and procedures for the course content and conduct from the first time they taught the classes to the present. These teaching examples operate at the intersections of communication, politics, and engineering education. When readers wonder how they might implement such courses at their own institutions, possibilities for transferability of key aspects are embedded in the chapters. For instance, when reflecting upon these chapters for learning, I thought that many readers of this edited collection would not have access to Ambassador Carolyn Curiel, Steve Scully, Brian Lamb, the infrastructure of EPICS, and other resources, but that they would have access to their local communities, the C-SPAN Archives, and regional political and cultural figures, as well as media specialists such as newscasters, bloggers, and so on. Where at first thought one might question how these courses could be replicated, the chapter authors have provided the details that open up opportunities to develop different but still highly interactive, project-based learning experiences with students and others. The hope here is that others engaged in learning and engagement find inspiration from these chapters to modify ideas to suit local needs and resources.

Finally, Roderick Hart's chapter was the result of an invitation to deliver the keynote address at the end of an NCA preconference on the C-SPAN Archives in Washington, DC, in 2013. The only request made was that he simply talk about C-SPAN and the C-SPAN Archives. What resulted was a talk so uplifting, so deceptively simple in its conversational style, but so complex and nuanced in content and eloquent that there could have been no better ending for the day. Bracketing his own personal reflections on the role that C-SPAN played in his life and that of his mother and other family members at the outset and conclusion of his chapter, Rod draws readers into political conversation and engagement. Moreover, he challenges readers to engage in the contestation of ideas and values at the heart of politics. He encourages examination of C-SPAN avoiders (i.e., "those desiring an antiseptic politics, politics without its affirmative passions"—namely "Web Evangelists" and "Uncivil Louts") and explication of their stances and arguments. He closes "Partisanship Without Alternatives: Keynote Reflections on C-SPAN and My Mother" by reminding readers of the following:

> Each day, C-SPAN tells us this story of politics and personality. How lucky we are that it does. My mother knew the glories of C-SPAN and she respected it profoundly. So do I. So should we all.

Roderick Hart's comments provide an apt ending to this edited collection and an apt beginning to further explorations in discovery, learning, and engagement that have been inspired by the women and men who contributed to this work on the C-SPAN Archives.

REFERENCES

Agran, L. (1984, September 4). *Grassroots '84, Mission Viejo* [C-SPAN online video]. Available from http://www.c-span.org/video/?48383-1/grassroots-84-mission-viejo

American Enterprise Institute for Public Policy Research (2007, April 30). *Civility and American politics: Conference summary.* Retrieved from http://www.aei.org/EMStaticPage/1510?page=Summary

Ansolabehere, S., & Stewart, C., III. (2009, January 1). Amazing race: How post-racial was Obama's victory? *Boston Review.* Retrieved from http://www.bostonreview.net/Ansolabehere-amazing-race

Austin, J. L., Urmson, J. O. (Ed.), & Sbisà, M. (Ed.). (1962). *How to do things with words: The William James Lectures delivered at Harvard University in 1955.* Oxford, UK: Clarendon.

Averill, J. R. (1980). A constructivist view of emotion. *Emotion: Theory, Research, and Experience, 1*, 305–339.

Baker, J. P. (1996). Prophecy, prophets. In I. H. Marshall, A. R. Millard, J. I. Packer, & D. J. Wiseman (Eds.), *New Bible dictionary* (3rd ed., pp. 964–975). Downers Grove, IL: InterVarsity Press.

Balz, D., & Cohen, J. (2007, February 28). Blacks shift to Obama, poll finds. *The Washington Post*. Retrieved from http://www.washingtonpost.com/wp-dyn/content/article/2007/02/27/AR2007022701030.html

Barker, D. C., & Carman, C. J. (2012). *Representing red and blue: How the culture wars change the way citizens speak and politicians listen*. New York, NY: Oxford University Press. http://dx.doi.org/10.1093/acprof:oso/9780199796564.001.0001

Barton, J. (2010, August 19). *Congressman Joe Barton town hall meeting* [C-SPAN online video]. Available from http://www.c-span.org/video/?295114-2/congressman-joe-barton-town-hall-meeting

Bateson, G. (1979). *Mind and nature: A necessary unity*. New York, NY: Ballantine Books.

Becker, A. (2008, May 23). Cable dot-coms add more content. *Broadcasting & Cable*. Retrieved from http://www.broadcastingcable.com/news/news-articles/cable-dot-coms-add-more-content/70861

Bell, J. (2012). *California crucible: The forging of modern American liberalism*. Philadelphia: University of Pennsylvania Press.

Bennis, W. (2007). The challenges of leadership in the modern world: Introduction to the special issue. *American Psychologist, 62*(1), 2–5. http://dx.doi.org/10.1037/0003-066X.62.1.2

Bergeson, M. (1984, September 5). *Grassroots '84* [C-SPAN online video]. Available from http://www.c-span.org/video/?48971-1/grassroots-84

Black, C. (1984, February 27). *New Hampshire primary* [C-SPAN online video]. Available from http://www.c-span.org/video/?98708-1/new-hampshire-primary

Bonner, J. (2010, August 26). *Congressman Jo Bonner town hall meeting* [C-SPAN online video]. Available from http://www.c-span.org/video/?295202-1/congressman-jo-bonner-town-hall-meeting

Bourdieu, P. (1986). Forms of capital. In J. Richardson (Ed.), *Handbook of theory and research for the sociology of education* (pp. 241–258). New York, NY: Greenwood Press.

Brader, T. (2011). The political relevance of emotions: "Reassessing" revisited. *Political Psychology, 32*(2), 337–346. http://dx.doi.org/10.1111/j.1467-9221.2010.00803.x

Bradley, B. (1993, September 2). *Senate town hall meeting* [C-SPAN online video]. Available from http://www.c-span.org/video/?49941-1/senate-town-hall-meeting

Brady, K. (2011, August 24). *Representative Kevin Brady town hall meeting* [C-SPAN online video]. Available from http://www.c-span.org/video/?301192-1/representative-kevin-brady-town-hall-meeting

Brinkley, A. (2010). Hoover and Roosevelt: Two approaches to leadership. In W. Isaacson (Ed.), Profiles in leadership: Historians on the elusive quality of greatness (pp. 187–208). New York, NY: W. W. Norton & Company.

Brooks, D. (2012, June 11). The follower problem. *The New York Times.* Retrieved from http://www.nytimes.com/2012/06/12/opinion/brooks-the-follower-problem.html?_r=1&hp#commentsContainer

Brossard, D., & Nisbet, M. C. (2007). Deference to scientific authority among a low information public: Understanding U.S. opinion on agricultural biotechnology. *International Journal of Public Opinion Research, 19*(1), 24–52. http://dx.doi.org/10.1093/ijpor/edl003

Brown, P., & Levinson, S. C. (1987). *Politeness: Some universals in language usage.* Cambridge, UK: Cambridge University Press.

Brownell, K. C. (2014). *Showbiz politics: Hollywood in American politics.* Chapel Hill: University of North Carolina Press.

Browning, R. X. (1992). Public affairs video archive: The C-SPAN Persian Gulf collection. *Film History, 22*(1), 57–62.

Bryan, F. M. (2003). *Real democracy: The New England town meeting and how it works.* Chicago, IL: University of Chicago Press. http://dx.doi.org/10.7208/chicago/9780226077987.001.0001

Buck, R. (1980). Nonverbal behavior and the theory of emotion: The facial feedback hypothesis. *Journal of Personality and Social Psychology, 38*(5), 811–824. http://dx.doi.org/10.1037/0022-3514.38.5.811

Burke, K. (1969). *A rhetoric of motives.* Berkeley: University of California Press.

Cantor, J. (1997, February 27). *Television ratings system* [C-SPAN online video]. Available from http://www.c-span.org/video/?79220-1/television-ratings-system

Chan-Olmsted, S. M., & Ha, L. S. (2003). Internet business models for broadcasters: How television stations perceive and integrate the Internet. *Journal of

Broadcasting & Electronic Media, 47(4), 597–616. http://dx.doi.org/10.1207/s15506878jobem4704_7

Chappell, D. L. (2005). *A stone of hope: Prophetic religion and the death of Jim Crow.* Chapel Hill: University of North Carolina Press.

Chicago Defender, The. (2010, March 23). Leaders discuss need for African American agenda. *The Chicago Defender.* Retrieved from http://www.chicagodefender.com/index.php/news/city/7549-leaders-discuss-need-for-african-american-agenda

Clayman, S. E., Elliott, M. N., Heritage, J., & McDonald, L. L. (2006). Historical trends in questioning presidents, 1953–2000. *Presidential Studies Quarterly, 36*(4), 561–583. http://dx.doi.org/10.1111/j.1741-5705.2006.02568.x

Clayman, S. E., & Heritage, J. (2002). Questioning presidents: Journalistic deference and adversarialness in the press conferences of U.S. presidents Eisenhower & Reagan. *Journal of Communication, 52*(4), 749–775. http://dx.doi.org/10.1111/j.1460-2466.2002.tb02572.x

Cmiel, K. (1990). *Democratic eloquence: The fight over popular speech in nineteenth-century America.* New York, NY: William Morrow and Company.

Coburn, T. (2011, August 16). *Senator Tom Coburn town hall meeting* [C-SPAN online video]. Available from http://www.c-span.org/video/?301062-1/senator-tom-coburn-town-hall-meeting

Coley, A. (2010, March 22). An open letter to Tavis Smiley. *CNN.* Retrieved from http://www.cnn.com/2010/OPINION/03/19/coley.obama.tavis.smiley/index.html

Colton, D. (1984, September 11). *Political polls* [C-SPAN online video]. Available from http://www.c-span.org/video/?48986-1/political-polls

Cone, J. H. (1997). *God of the oppressed.* Maryknoll, NY: Orbis Books.

Cooper, H. (2010, February 10). Black leaders push Obama for jobs bill. *The New York Times.* Retrieved from http://www.nytimes.com/2010/02/11/us/politics/11obama.html

Cummings, E. (2009, August 3). *Veterans town hall meeting* [C-SPAN online video]. Available from http://www.c-span.org/video/?288199-1/veterans-town-hall-meeting

Cummins, D., & Bindel, J. (2007, December 5). Mills & Boon: 100 years of heaven or hell? *The Guardian.* Retrieved from http://www.guardian.co.uk/lifeandstyle/2007/dec/05/women.fiction

Darsey, J. (1999). *The prophetic tradition and radical rhetoric in America*. New York, NY: New York University Press.

Democratic National Committee. (1984, July 16). *Democratic National Convention day 1* [C-SPAN online video]. Available from http://www.c-span.org/video/?124426-1/democratic-national-convention-day-1

Disch, L. (2012). Democratic representation and the constituency paradox. *Perspectives on Politics, 10*(3), 599–616. http://dx.doi.org/10.1017/S1537592712001636

Dochuk, D. (2010). *From Bible belt to sunbelt: Plain folk religion, grassroots politics, and the rise of evangelical conservatism*. New York, NY: W. W. Norton.

Donnerstein, E. (1993, October 20). *Violence in television programming* [C-SPAN online video]. Available from http://www.c-span.org/video/?51691-1/violence-television-programming

Douglas, S. (2012, October). *The presidency, media affordances and media aptitudes*. Paper presented on the panel "Presidents and the Media" at the Recasting Presidential History Conference, Miller Center for Public Affairs, Charlottesville, VA.

Drash, W. (2009, January 12). Grandson of slaves: Obama is our Moses. *CNN*. Retrieved from http://www.cnn.com/2009/US/01/12/grandson.of.slaves/index.html

Drew, P., & Heritage, J. (1992). Analyzing talk at work: An introduction. In P. Drew & J. Heritage (Eds.), *Talk at work: Interaction in institutional settings* (pp. 3–65). New York, NY: Cambridge University Press.

Duncan, H. D. (1985). *Communication and social order*. New Brunswick, NJ: Transaction Books.

Ekman, P. (1970). Universal facial expressions of emotion. *California Mental Health Research Digest, 8*(4), 151–158.

Ekman, P. (1999). Basic emotions. In T. Dalgleish & M. J. Power (Eds.), *Handbook of cognition and emotion* (pp. 45–60). New York, NY: John Wiley & Sons Ltd.

Ekman, P. (2003). *Emotions revealed: Recognizing faces and feelings to improve communication and emotional life*. New York, NY: Henry Holt.

EPICS/Purdue (n.d.). Camp Riley (CR). Retrieved from https://engineering.purdue.edu/EPICS/Projects/Teams/viewTeam?teamid=79

EPICS/Purdue (2014). Join us—The Habitat for Humanity EPICS team. Retrieved from http://epics.ecn.purdue.edu/hfh/

Feiler, B. (2009). *America's prophet: Moses and the American story*. New York, NY: HarperCollins.

Feingold, R. (1993, April 16). *Wisconsin town hall meeting* [C-SPAN online video]. Available from http://www.c-span.org/video/?39784-1/wisconsin-town-hall-meeting

Fischer, A. H. (Ed.). (2000). *Gender and emotion: Social psychological perspectives*. Cambridge, UK: Cambridge University Press.

Fenno, R. F., Jr. (1978). *Home style: House members in their districts*. New York, NY: HarperCollins.

Flyvbjerg, B. (2001). *Making social science matter: Why social inquiry fails and how it can succeed again*. Cambridge, UK: Cambridge University Press. http://dx.doi.org/10.1017/CBO9780511810503

Frantzich, S., & Sullivan, J. (1996). *The C-SPAN revolution*. Norman: University of Oklahoma Press.

Freeman, L. C. (1977). A set of measures of centrality based on betweenness. *Sociometry, 40*(1), 35–41. http://dx.doi.org/10.2307/3033543

Friedman, T. L. (2011, October 8). Where have you gone, Joe DiMaggio? *The New York Times*. Retrieved from http://www.nytimes.com/2011/10/09/opinion/sunday/friedman-where-have-you-gone-joe-dimaggio.html?smid=pl-share

Garrow, D. J. (1986). *Bearing the cross: Martin Luther King, Jr., and the Southern Christian Leadership Conference*. New York, NY: Harper Collins.

Gastil, J. (1994). A definition and illustration of democratic leadership. *Human Relations, 47*(8), 953–975. http://dx.doi.org/10.1177/001872679404700805

Geer, J. G. (1996). *From tea leaves to opinion polls: A theory of democratic leadership*. New York, NY: Columbia University Press.

Geertz, C. (2001). Empowering Aristotle. *Science, 293*(5527), 53. http://dx.doi.org/10.1126/science.1062054

Geismer, L. (2014). *Don't blame us: Suburban liberals and the transformation of the Democratic Party*. Princeton, NJ: Princeton University Press.

Gingrich, N. (1998, October 19). *Georgia town hall meeting* [C-SPAN online video]. Available from http://www.c-span.org/video/?114051-1/georgia-town-hall-meeting

Gitell, S. (2008, January 8). Is Obama like King? *The New York Sun*. Retrieved from http://www.nysun.com/opinion/is-obama-like-king/69072/

Gitlin, T. (1990). Blips, bites, and savvy talk. In N. Mills (Ed.), *Culture in an age of money* (pp. 29–46). New York, NY: Ivan R. Dee.

Glaude, E. S., Jr. (2012). Religion and violence in black and white. In J. D. Carlson & J. H. Ebel (Eds.), *From Jeremiad to Jihad: Religion, violence, and America* (pp. 128–142). Berkeley: University of California Press.

Goffman, E. (1956). The nature of deference and demeanor. *American Anthropologist, 58*(3), 473–502. http://dx.doi.org/10.1525/aa.1956.58.3.02a00070

Goffman, E. (1959). *The presentation of self in everyday life*. New York, NY: Doubleday Anchor Books.

Grassley, C. (2009, August 12). *Senator Grassley town hall meeting* [C-SPAN online video]. Available from http://www.c-span.org/video/?288345-1/senator-grassley-town-hall-meeting

Greenberg, D. (2004). *Nixon's shadow: The history of an image*. New York, NY: W. W. Norton.

Greenberg, D. (2012). Do historians watch enough TV? Broadcast news as a primary source. In C. B. Potter & R. C. Romano (Eds.), *Doing recent history: On privacy, copyright, video games, institutional review boards, activist scholarship, and history that talks back* (pp. 185–199). Athens: The University of Georgia Press.

Greer, C. F., & Ferguson, D. A. (2011). Using Twitter for promotion and branding: A content analysis of local television Twitter sites. *Journal of Broadcasting & Electronic Media, 55*(2), 198–214. http://dx.doi.org/10.1080/08838151.2011.570824

Han, S.-H., & Brazeal, L. M. (2013, April). *I 'respectfully' disagree: The effects of news framing on civility in political discussion*. Paper presented at the Central States Communication Association 2013 Convention, Kansas City, MO.

Hansen, D. L., Schneiderman, B., & Smith, M. A. (2010). *Analyzing social media networks with NodeXL insights from a connected world*. Retrieved from http://www.sciencedirect.com/science/book/9780123822291

Harris, F. C. (2012, October 27). The price of a Black president. *The New York Times*. Retrieved from http://www.nytimes.com/2012/10/28/opinion/sunday/the-price-of-a-black-president.html?pagewanted=all&_r=2&

Harris, H. R. (2010, March 19). It's Sharpton vs. Jackson on Smiley vs. Obama. *Washington Post*. Retrieved from http://voices.washingtonpost.com/44/2010/03/its-sharpton-vs-jackson-on-smi.html

Hart, R. P. (1999). *Seducing America: How television charms the modern voter* (Rev. ed.). Thousand Oaks, CA: SAGE Publications.

Hawthorne, C. (2008, August 30). Obama turns to Greek columns for support. *Los Angeles Times*. Retrieved from http://www.latimes.com/entertainment/news/arts/la-et-notebook30-2008aug30,0,1912209.story

Heschel, A. J. (2010). *The prophets*. Peabody, MA: Hendrickson Publishers.

Hohmann, J. (2010, February 21). Alexander Haig, 85; soldier-statesman managed Nixon resignation. *Washington Post*. Retrieved from http://www.washingtonpost.com/wp-dyn/content/story/2010/02/20/ST2010022001340.html?sid=ST2010022001340

Houser, J. A., & Lovaglia, M. J. (2002). Status, emotion and the development of solidarity in stratified task groups. In S. R. Thye & E. J. Lawler (Eds.), *Group cohesion, trust and solidarity* (pp. 109–137). Bingley, UK: Emerald Group Publishing Limited.

Hutchinson, E. O. (2010, March 9). Good reason Blacks give Obama a racial pass. *The Chicago Defender*. Retrieved from http://www.chicagodefender.com/index.php/voices/7633-good-reason-blacks-give-obama-a-racial-pass

Istook, E. (1992, August 24). *Oklahoma House race* [C-SPAN online video]. Available from http://www.c-span.org/video/?31511-1/oklahoma-house-race

Jacobs, M., & Zelizer, J. (2011). *Conservatives in power: The Reagan years, 1981–1989: A brief history with documents*. Boston, MA: Bedford/St. Martin.

Jacobson, G. C. (2013). Partisan polarization in American politics: A background paper. *Presidential Studies Quarterly, 43*(4), 688–708. http://dx.doi.org/10.1111/psq.12062

James, M. (2009, March 18). Bust of MLK joins President Obama in Oval Office. *ABC News*. Retrieved from http://abcnews.go.com/blogs/politics/2009/03/bust-of-mlk-joi/

Jamieson, K. H. (1996). *Packaging the presidency: A history and criticism of presidential campaign advertising* (3rd ed.). New York, NY: Oxford University Press.

Jamieson, K. H. (1997). *Civility in the House of Representatives: A background report*. State College: University of Pennsylvania, Annenberg Public Policy Center.

Jaroslovsky, R. (1984, September 7). *Grassroots '84* [C-SPAN online video]. Available from http://www.c-span.org/video/?48974-1/grassroots-84

Jasper County Democratic Party. (1984, February 20). *Iowa rural caucus* [C-SPAN online video]. Available from http://www.c-span.org/video/?124894-1/iowa-rural-caucus

Joint Select Committee. (2011, November 1). *Joint Select Committee on Deficit Reduction hearing* [C-SPAN online video]. Available from http://C-SPANvideo.org/topic/85

Kane, J., & Patapan, H. (2010). The artless art: Leadership and the limits of democratic rhetoric. *Australian Journal of Political Science, 45*(3), 371–389. http://dx.doi.org/10.1080/10361146.2010.499162

Kay, J. (2012, November). *Community-building and ritual: The town hall as a political campaign strategy*. Paper presented at National Communication Association 98th annual convention, Orlando, FL.

Kellerman, B. (1984). *The political presidency: Practice of leadership*. New York, NY: Oxford University Press.

Kerrey, B. (1993, August 28). *Nebraska senatorial town meeting* [C-SPAN online video]. Available from http://www.c-span.org/video/?49567-1/nebraska-senatorial-town-meeting

Kirwan Institute (2010a). *Beyond the quick fix: ARRA contracting, jobs, and building a fair recovery for Florida*. Retrieved from http://www.gis.kirwaninstitute.org/reports/2010/01_2010_FL_ARRAContractingEquity.pdf

Kirwan Institute (2010b). *Race-recovery index: Is stimulus helping communities in crisis?* Retrieved from http://www.gis.kirwaninstitute.org/reports/2010/02_2010_RaceRecoveryIndex.pdf

Klein, J. (2009). The character question. *Time, 174*(11), 24.

Kolers, A. (2005). Justice and the politics of deference. *Journal of Political Philosophy, 13*(2), 153–173. http://dx.doi.org/10.1111/j.1467-9760.2005.00218.x

Kruse, K. (2007). *White flight and the making of modern conservatism*. Princeton, NJ: Princeton University Press.

Lamb, B. (1984, November 5). *Week in review* [C-SPAN online video]. Available from http://www.c-span.org/video/?101475-1/week-review

Lamprey, S. (1984, February 22). *New Hampshire primary* [C-SPAN online video]. Available from http://www.c-span.org/video/?72096-1/new-hampshire-primary

Lassiter, M. (2006). *The silent majority: Suburban politics in the Sunbelt south*. Princeton, NJ: Princeton University Press.

Lee, B. (2007, March 24). *Town hall meeting on the war in Iraq* [C-SPAN online video].

Available from http://www.c-span.org/video/?197320-1/town-hall-meeting-war-iraq

Lee, M. (2011, August 30). *Senator Mike Lee town hall meeting* [C-SPAN online video]. Available from http://www.c-span.org/video/?301297-1/senator-mike-lee-town-hall-meeting

Lees-Marshment, J. (2012). Political marketing and opinion leadership: Comparative perspectives and findings. In L. Helms (Ed.), *Comparative political leadership* (pp. 165–185) [Palgrave Connect version]. http://dx.doi.org/10.1057/9781137264916.0011

Li, E. Y., Liao, C. H., & Yen, H. R. (2013). Co-authorship networks and research impact: A social capital perspective. *Research Policy, 42*(9), 1515–1530. http://dx.doi.org/10.1016/j.respol.2013.06.012

Lieberman, J. (1999, March 31). *Town hall meeting on Social Security* [C-SPAN online video]. Available from http://www.c-span.org/video/?122230-1/town-hall-meeting-social-security

Lott, T. (1993, August 30). *Senator Lott town hall meeting* [C-SPAN online video]. Available from http://www.c-span.org/video/?49940-1/senator-lott-town-hall-meeting

Lungren, D. (2009, August 18). *Representative Dan Lungren town hall meeting* [online video]. Available from http://www.c-span.org/video/?288451-1/representative-dan-lungren-town-hall-meeting

Marcus, G. E. (2000). Emotions in politics. *Annual Review of Political Science, 3*(1), 221–250. http://dx.doi.org/10.1146/annurev.polisci.3.1.221

Martin, B. (2011). *The other eighties: A secret history of America in the age of Reagan.* New York, NY: Hill and Wang.

Martin, R. S. (2010, April 9). Confederates, Al-Qaida are the same: Terrorists [Web log post]. Retrieved from http://www.rolandsmartin.com/blog/index.php/2010/04/09/confederates-al-qaida-are-the-same-terrorists

Matei, S. A., Bertino, E., Zhu, M., Liu, C., Si, L., & Britt, B. (2014). A research agenda for the study of entropic social structural evolution, functional roles, adhocratic leadership styles, and credibility in online organizations and knowledge markets. In E. Bertino & S. A. Matei (Eds.), *Roles, trust, and reputation in social media knowledge markets: Theory and methods.* New York, NY: Springer.

McGirr, L. (2002). *Suburban warriors: The origins of the new American right.* Princeton, NJ: Princeton University Press.

Meek, C. (1992, September 24). *Day in the life of Representative Meek* [C-SPAN online video]. Available from http://www.c-span.org/video/?33555-1/day-life-representative-meek

Mehrabian, A., & Ferris, S. R. (1967). Inference of attitudes from nonverbal communication in two channels. *Journal of Consulting Psychology, 31*(3), 248–252. http://dx.doi.org/10.1037/h0024648

Mercieca, J. R. (2010). *Founding fictions.* Tuscaloosa: University of Alabama Press.

Mikulski, B., & Sarbanes, P. (1999, September 27). *Health care town hall meeting* [C-SPAN online video]. Available from http://www.c-span.org/video/?152388-1/health-care-town-hall-meeting

Milligan, S. (2011, April 5). Paul Ryan ignores polls, shows leadership in budget debate. *U.S. News & World Report.* Retrieved from http://www.usnews.com/opinion/blogs/susan-milligan/2011/04/05/paul-ryan-ignores-polls-shows-leadership-in-budget-debate

Murkowski, L. (2009, August 20). *Senator Murkowski town hall meeting* [C-SPAN online video]. Available from http://www.c-span.org/video/?288485-1/senator-murkowski-town-hall-meeting

Murphy, J. M. (2011). Barack Obama, the Exodus tradition, and the Joshua generation. *Quarterly Journal of Speech, 97*(4), 387–410. http://dx.doi.org/10.1080/00335630.2011.608706

Myers, D., & Tingley, D. (2011). *The influence of emotion on trust* [Report]. Retrieved from scholar.harvard.edu/files/dtingley/files/emotionmanipulationm11.pdf

National Public Radio (2010, March 12). *Congressional Black Caucus member discusses Obama meeting* [Recording with transcript]. Retrieved from http://www.npr.org/templates/story/story.php?storyId=124623729

O'Reilly, T. (2005, September 30). What is Web 2.0: Design patterns and business models for the next generation of software [Web log post]. Retrieved from http://www.oreilly.com/pub/a/oreilly/tim/news/2005/09/30/what-is-web-20.html

Padgett, T. (2009, November 23). Are minorities being fleeced by the stimulus? *Time.* Retrieved from http://www.time.com/time/nation/article/0,8599,1940338,00.html

Pence, M. (2010, January 7). *Representative Mike Pence town hall meeting* [C-SPAN online video]. Available from http://www.c-span.org/video/?291235-1/representative-mike-pence-town-hall-meeting

Pew Research Center (2011, September 22). Press widely criticized, but trusted more than other information sources. Retrieved from http://www.people-press.org/2011/09/22/press-widely-criticized-but-trusted-more-than-other-institutions/

Phillips-Fein, K. (2009). *Invisible hands: The businessmen's crusade against the New Deal*. New York, NY: W. W. Norton.

Phillips-Fein, K. (2011). Conservatism: A state of the field. *Journal of American History, 98*(3), 723–743. http://dx.doi.org/10.1093/jahist/jar430

Pitkin, H. F. (1967). *The concept of representation*. Berkeley: University of California Press.

Platt, E. (1992). Pedagogical uses 2: The Gulf, the media, and the classroom—The C-SPAN advantage. *Film History, 22*(1), 52–56.

Raboteau, A. J. (1994). African-Americans, Exodus, and the American Israel. In P. E. Johnson (Ed.), *African-American Christianity: Essays in history* (pp. 1–17). Berkeley: University of California Press.

Republican National Committee (1984, August 20). *Republican National Convention day 1* [C-SPAN online video]. Available from http://www.c-span.org/video/?124531-1/republican-national-convention-day-1

Rothenbuhler, E. W. (1998). *Ritual communication: From everyday conversation to mediated ceremony*. Thousand Oaks, CA: Sage Publications.

Rucker, P. (2009, August 11). Specter faces raucous crowd at town hall meeting. *The Washington Post*. Retrieved from http://www.washingtonpost.com/wp-dyn/content/article/2009/08/11/AR2009081101880.html

Russell, J. A. & Fernández-Dols, J. M. (Eds.). (1997). *The psychology of facial expression* [Cambridge Books Online version]. http://dx.doi.org/10.1017/CBO9780511659911

Rustin, B. (1965, February 1). From protests to politics: The future of the civil rights movement. *Commentary*. Retrieved from http://www.commentarymagazine.com/article/from-protest-to-politics-the-future-of-the-civil-rights-movement/

Ryfe, D. M. (2001). Presidential communication as cultural form: The town hall meeting. In R. P. Hart & B. H. Sparrow (Eds.), *Politics, discourse, and American society: New agendas* (pp. 173–192). Lanham, MD: Rowman & Littlefield Publishers.

Sasser, B. (2006, June 12). Locking out New Orleans' poor. *Salon Magazine*. Retrieved from http://www.salon.com/news/feature/2006/06/12/nola_housing

Sears, D. O. (1993). Symbolic politics: A socio-psychological theory. In S. Lyengar & W. J. McGuire (Eds.), *Explorations in political psychology* (pp. 113–149). Durham, NC: Duke University Press.

Sears, D. O., & Chaffee, S. H. (1979). Uses and effects of the 1976 debates: An overview of empirical studies. In S. Kraus (Ed.), *The great debates: Carter vs. Ford, 1976* (pp. 223–261). Bloomington: Indiana University Press.

Sears, D. O., & Citrin, J. (1982). *Tax revolt: Something for nothing in California.* Cambridge, MA: Harvard University Press.

Selby, G. S. (2008). *Martin Luther King and the rhetoric of freedom: The Exodus narrative in America's struggle for civil rights.* Waco, TX: Baylor University Press.

Seymour, J., & Torres, A. (1984, September 5). *Reagan's presidential campaign* [C-SPAN online video]. Available from http://www.c-span.org/video/?123807-1/reagans-presidential-campaign

Shamir, B. (2013). Notes on distance and leadership. In M. C. Bligh & R. E. Riggio (Eds.), *Exploring distance in leader-follower relationships: When near is far and far is near* (pp. 39–60). New York, NY: Routledge.

Shelly, G., & Frydenberg, M. (2010). *Web 2.0: Concepts and applications.* Boston, MA: Cengage Learning.

Shields, S. A., & MacDowell, K. A. (1987). "Appropriate" emotion in politics: Judgments of a televised debate. *Journal of Communication, 37*(2), 78–89. http://dx.doi.org/10.1111/j.1460-2466.1987.tb00984.x

Simons, H. W., & Leibowitz, K. (1979). Shifts in candidate images. In S. Kraus (Ed.), *The great debates: Carter vs. Ford, 1976* (pp. 398–404). Bloomington: Indiana University Press.

Smiley, T. (2010, March 20). *Tavis Smiley Black agenda forum* [C-SPAN online video]. Available from http://www.c-span.org/video/?292635-7/tavis-smiley-black-agenda-forum

Smiley, T. (2013, January 20). Tavis Smiley on Obama and MLK's legacy. Retrieved from http://www.cbsnews.com/8301-3445_162-57564890/tavis-smiley-on-obama-and-mlks-legacy/

Smith, K. K. (1999). *The dominion of voice: Riot, reason, and antebellum politics.* Lawrence: University of Kansas.

Smith, Z. (2011). *From the well of the House: Remaking the Republican Party from 1978 to 1994* (Unpublished doctoral dissertation). Boston University, Boston, MA.

Solomon, R. C. (1976). *The passions: Emotions and the meaning of life.* Indianapolis, IN: Hackett Publishing.

Sound judgment: Murkowski broke filibuster, but voted against Jones. (2013 August 9). *Fairbanks Daily News-Miner.* Retrieved from http://m.newsminer.com/opinion/editorials/sound-judgment-murkowski-broke-filibuster-but-voted-against-jones/article_1cf3a904-00b2-11e3-ac7d-001a4bcf6878.html?mode=jqm

Sparks, G. G. (2013). *Mass communication research: A basic overview.* Boston, MA: Wadsworth.

Stelter, B. (2010, March 16). C-SPAN puts full archives on the Web. *The New York Times.* Retrieved from http://www.nytimes.com/2010/03/16/arts/television/16cspan.html

Stembergh, A. (2006, October 8). Stephen Colbert has America by the ballots. *New York Magazine.* Retrieved from http://nymag.com/news/politics/22322/

Stolberg, S. G. (2010, February 8). For Obama, nuance on race invites questions. *The New York Times.* Retrieved from http://www.nytimes.com/2010/02/09/us/politics/09race.html

Stupak, B. (2010, January 7). *Representative Stupak town hall meeting* [C-SPAN online video]. Available from http://www.c-span.org/video/?291233-1/representative-stupak-town-hall-meeting

Sugrue, T. (2003). All politics is local: The persistence of localism in twentieth-century America. In M. Jacobs, W. Novak, & J. Zelizer (Eds.), *The democratic experiment: New directions in American political history* (pp. 301–326). Princeton, NJ: Princeton University Press.

Summers, M. (1984, February 21). *New Hampshire primary* [C-SPAN online video]. Available from http://www.c-span.org/video/?72090-1/new-hampshire-primary

Taber, C. S., & Lodge, M. (2006). Motivated skepticism in the evaluation of political beliefs. *American Journal of Political Science, 50*(3), 755–769. http://dx.doi.org/10.1111/j.1540-5907.2006.00214.x

Tannenbaum, P. H., Greenberg, B. S., & Silverman, F. R. (1962). Candidate images. In S. Kraus (Ed.), *The great debates: Carter vs. Ford, 1976* (pp. 271–288). Bloomington: Indiana University Press.

Terry, D. (2010, March 19). A delicate balancing act for the Black agenda. *The New York Times.* Retrieved from http://www.nytimes.com/2010/03/19/us/19cncagenda.html

Townsend, R. M. (2009). Town meeting as a communication event: Democracy's act sequence. *Research on Language and Social Interaction, 42*(1), 68–89. http://dx.doi.org/10.1080/08351810802671743

Tough, P. (2012, August 15). What does Obama really believe in? *The New York Times.* Retrieved from http://www.nytimes.com/2012/08/19/magazine/obama-poverty.html

Troy, G. (2005). *Morning in America: How Ronald Reagan invented the 1980s.* Princeton, NJ: Princeton University Press.

Tulis, J. K. (1987). *The rhetorical presidency.* Princeton, NJ: Princeton University Press.

Urbina, I. (2009, August 7). Beyond beltway, health care debate turns hostile. *The New York Times.* Retrieved from http://www.nytimes.com/2009/08/08/us/politics/08townhall.html?_r=0

Wagner, H. L. (1997). Methods for the study of facial behavior. In J. Russell & J. M. Fernández-Dols (Eds.), *The psychology of facial expression* (pp. 31–54). New York, NY: Cambridge University Press. http://dx.doi.org/10.1017/CBO9780511659911.004

West, C. (1993). *Prophetic fragments: Illuminations of the crisis in American religion and culture.* Grand Rapids, MI: William B. Eerdmans Publishing Company.

West, C. (2002). *Prophesy deliverance!* Louisville, KY: Westminster John Knox Press.

West, C. (2011, August 25). Dr. King weeps from his grave. *The New York Times.* Retrieved from http://www.nytimes.com/2011/08/26/opinion/martin-luther-king-jr-would-want-a-revolution-not-a-memorial.html

Wickham, D. (2010, March 3). What should Obama do for Blacks? First, heal a growing rift. *USA Today.* Retrieved from http://usatoday30.usatoday.com/NEWS/usaedition/2010-03-02-column02_ST1_U.htm

Wilentz, S. (2008). *The age of Reagan: A history, 1974–2008.* New York, NY: Harper Collins Publisher.

Wolfe, T. (1999, February 25). *Marshall McLuhan lecture* [C-SPAN online video]. Available from http://www.c-span.org/video/?120940-1/marshall-mcluhan-lecture

Wyden, R. (2010, January 10). *Senator Ron Wyden town hall meeting* [C-SPAN online video]. Available from http://www.c-span.org/video/?291183-1/senator-ron-wyden-town-hall-meeting

Zelizer, J. E. (2012). *Governing America: The revival of political history.* Princeton, NJ: Princeton University Press.

CONTRIBUTORS

Stephanie E. Bor is an assistant professor in the Reynolds School of Journalism at the University of Nevada Reno. Her research examines the intersection of digital media, politics, and organizational communication. She has been conducting research with C-SPAN since 2012, when she was awarded the Scripps Howard Foundation/Association for Education in Journalism and Mass Communication (AEJMC) Social Media Faculty Grant for social media journalism education research.

Kathryn Cramer Brownell is assistant professor of history at Purdue University. Her research and teaching focus on the relationships between media, politics, and popular culture in 20th-century United States. She is the author of *Showbiz Politics: Hollywood in American Political Life* (University of North Carolina Press, 2014), which explores the institutionalization of Hollywood styles and structures in American politics over the course of the 20th century. She has also published articles in *The Moving Image* and *Journal of Policy History* and has a forthcoming chapter, "The Making of the Celebrity Presidency" in Brian Balogh and Bruce Schulman, eds., *Recasting Presidential History* (Cornell University Press, forthcoming 2015).

Robert X. Browning is an associate professor of political science and of communication in the Brian Lamb School of Communication at Purdue University. In 1987, he became the founding director of the C-SPAN Archives. He is the author of *Politics and Social Welfare Policy in the United States* and papers on redistricting. Awarded the George Foster Peabody Award for its online Video Library in 2010, the C-SPAN Archives is housed in the Purdue Research Park and offers a window into American life.

Patrice M. Buzzanell is a professor in the Brian Lamb School of Communication and the School of Engineering Education (by courtesy) at Purdue University. She is the editor of 3 books and the author of more than 150 articles and chapters. Her research centers on the intersections of career, gender, and communication and has appeared in such journals as *Human Relations, Communication Monographs, Management Communication Quarterly, Communication Theory, Human Communication Research,* and *Journal of Applied Communication Research,* as well as proceedings for the American Society for Engineering Education and Frontiers in Education. Fellow and past president of the International Communication Association, Dr. Buzzanell also has served as president of the Council of Communication Associations and the Organization for the Study of Communication, Language and Gender. In 2010 she delivered the Carroll C. Arnold Distinguished Lecture, "Seduction and Sustainability: The Politics of Feminist Communication and Career Scholarship," to the National Communication Association. Most recently, she is the 2014 recipient of the Provost's Outstanding Graduate Mentor Award at Purdue.

Roderick P. Hart holds the Shivers Chair in Communication and is professor of government at the University of Texas at Austin, where he also serves as dean of the Moody College of Communication and where he was founding director of the Annette Strauss Institute for Civic Life. He is the author or editor of 12 books, the most recent of which is *Political Tone: What Leaders Say and Why* (University of Chicago Press, 2014). Dr. Hart has been named a Fellow of the International Communication Association, a Distinguished Scholar by the National Communication Association, and received the Edelman Career Award from the American Political Science Association. He is also a member of the Academy of Distinguished Teachers at UT Austin.

Theon E. Hill is an assistant professor of communication at Wheaton College. His research explores the relationship between rhetoric and social change. Specifically, he examines the role of radical rhetoric as a crucial form of civic engagement and public advocacy. His previous work on rhetoric and social change in political, social movement, and religious contexts has appeared in edited collections and scholarly journals. Currently, he is working on a book-length manuscript examining the relevance of Martin Luther King Jr. in the age of Obama.

Christopher Kowal is an assistant professor in the Department of Consumer Science and the director of the Center for Professional Selling at Purdue University. He earned his BA in communication and political science from Oakland University in Rochester, Michigan, MA from the University of Connecticut, and PhD degree from the University of Connecticut in communication and marketing, with a focus on the communication of emotions within persuasion. Dr. Kowal's research focus is in nonverbal communication, specifically the persuasion of emotion, exploring the process of charisma, and emotional competence.

Colene J. Lind is assistant professor and graduate studies director in the Department of Communication Studies at Kansas State University. She studies political language, culture, and leadership. She co-authored *Political Tone: How Leaders Talk and Why* (Chicago, 2013) with Roderick P. Hart and Jay P. Childers.

Sorin Adam Matei is associate professor of communication in the Brian Lamb School of Communication and director of research for computational social science in the Cyber Center at Purdue University. He works with his students and colleagues on creating new Web-enabled tools for fostering equitable leadership and self-management procedures and tools, especially for learning and creative virtual communities. Dr. Matei has published papers and developed software that aim to make these a reality. Among the tools and sites he has created are KredibleNet (http://kredible.net), Matei.org Ithink (http://matei.org/ithink), Visible Effort (http://veffort.us), AlterPode (alterpode.com), and Visible Past (http://visiblepast.net). He is the coeditor of the book *Roles, Trust, and Reputation in Social Media Knowledge Markets: Theories and Methods* (Spinger, 2014).

William Oakes is the director of Engineering Projects in Community Service (EPICS) and professor of engineering education at Purdue University. He has devoted much of his career to the dissemination of engineering-centered community engagement at the university and K–12 level by conducting faculty and teacher professional development workshops and publishing conference and journal articles and books, including coauthoring the first text for engineering service-learning. He has received numerous awards for his efforts, including being the first engineer to receive the U.S. Campus Compact Thomas Ehrlich Faculty Award, a corecipient of the U.S. National Academy of Engineering's Bernard Gordon Prize for Innovation in Engineering and Technology Education, and the recipient of the U.S. National Society of Professional Engineers' Educational Excellence Award. He is a fellow of the American Society for Engineering Education and the National Society of Professional Engineers.

Glenn G. Sparks has been a professor of communication at Purdue University since 1986. He served as the associate head of what is now the Brian Lamb School of Communication for 12 years (2001–2013). He conducts research and teaches courses in communication theory, the theory and effects of mass media, relationships in the electronic era, and research methods. He is the author of *Media Effects Research: A Basic Overview*, an undergraduate text in its 5th edition. He is also a coauthor of *A First Look at Communication Theory*, a text designed to introduce students to theory in communication.

Carla B. Zoltowski is codirector of Engineering Projects in Community Service (EPICS) at Purdue University and is responsible for teaching design and developing curriculum and assessment tools for the program. She has conducted qualitative and mixed-methods research and is co-principal investigator on two National Science Foundation studies related to engineering ethics.

INDEX

Page numbers in italics refer to figures.

A
ABC, 21
Abramoff lobbying scandal, 5
Academic-community partnerships, xvi–xvii, 3, 5
Accommodation, 69–72
Accuracy of news, perceived, 85–86, 90
Advanced analytics, 96–98
Affordable Care Act, 5
  town hall meetings on, 59–61
Afghanistan War, 5

African Americans
  as Israel, 40–42
  black political agency, 29–30, 39–40
  discontent in the age of Obama, 31–33
  election of Barack Obama and, 29–30
  Obama as Moses and, 29, 33, 35–37
  poverty rates, 32–33
  "We Count! The Black Agenda is the American Agenda," 30, 33–34

Agran, Larry, 53
Allen, Thad, 142
Amazon Web Services, 8
Ambrose, Stephen, 165
American government concepts. *See also* Leadership; Politics
  members of Congress lobbying for committee assignments, 136–138
  partisanship, 155–158
  party identification and, 134–135
  student assignments using C-SPAN video, 138
  value of C-SPAN videos in teaching, 139–140
American History TV, 5
American Majority, 101
American Reinvestment and Recovery Act, 31
Analytics, advanced, 96–98
Anger, 100
Application programming interface (API), 117–119
Appreciation, 65–69
Arab Spring, 5
Asymmetric versus mutual deference, 72–75
Austin, J. L., 164

B

Bacon, Joel, xx
Bailey, Doug, 160
Balz, Dan, 143
Barker, D. C., 63, 74
Barton, Joe, 74
Beck, Glenn, 167n3
Bell, J., 58n4, 58n5
Bennis, Warren, 73–74
Bergman, Teresa, xx
Big data, 109
Bill Daniels Fund, 141
Bisson, Charles, 102
Black, C., 57n3
Black political agency, 39–40. *See also* African Americans
  African Americans as Israel and, 40
  defined, 29–30
Blackwell, Angela Glover, 33
Bledsoe, Woody, 102–103, 105
Blitzer, Wolf, 21
Blogs, 11
Bloomberg View, 142
Bonner, J., 66
BookTV, 5
Boortz, Neal, 166
Bor, Stephanie, 13, 174
Bork, Robert, 5
Bourdieu, P., 112
Bradley, Bill, 60
Brady, Kevin, 68–69, 70
Breyer, Stephen, 24
Brian Lamb School of Communication, xx, 3, 6, 124–125, 131
  Purdue Institute for Civic Communication (PICC), 141–142
Brinkley, Alan, 63
Broadcast television, 21, 48, 81
Brownell, Kathryn Cramer, 12, 58n5, 173
Browning, Robert, xiii, ix, 15, 19, 82, 170, 175

Browning, Robert *(continued)*
   C-SPAN Video Library system creation, 3–6
   Engineering Programs in the Community (EPICS) and, 148
Bryan, Frank, 60
Buddenhagen, Kristina, xx
Burke, Edmund, 63
Burrell, Tom, 34
Buzzanell, Patrice, xiii, ix, 6
   on importance of C-SPAN Archives, 169–171
   reflections on chapter contributions, 171–177

C

Cable Satellite Public Affairs Network. *See* C-SPAN
Cable television, 17–18, 48–49
Caddell, Pat, 143
Camp Riley (CR), 146
Cantor, Joanne, *128*, 128–129, *132*
Caplan, Craig, 87
Caputo, David, xxi, 4
Carlson, Margaret, 142
Carman, C. J., 63, 74
Carrick, Kenneth, xx
Carter, Jimmy, 49, 144
CBS, 21
Charisma, 99
Christian Broadcasting Network, 17
Citizen initiative, 69–70
Clayman, Steve, 69
Clinton, Bill, 24, 53
   accused of governing by polls, 64
   emotions shown by, 99
   impeachment of, 5, 100
Clipping and sharing of video, 10–12, 134
Closed captioning, 9–10
Clyburn, William, 117
CNN, 18, 21, 167n3
Coburn, Tom, 68
Cognition, need for, 99
Cold War, 5
Colton, David, 51
Columbia, space shuttle, 5
Columbine school shooting, 5
Comedy Central, 167n3
Committee assignments, congressional, 136–138
Congressional Black Caucus, 32
Congressional Budget Office, 117
Congressional Record, 10, 94
Coyle, Ed, 148
C-SPAN
   access to content on, 19–20, 81–82
   advanced analytics and, 96–98
   beginnings of, 4, 16, 48–49
   as centrality in politics, 166–167
   coverage of 1984 presidential election, 47–48
   coverage of town hall meetings, 60–61, 76
   debate metadata analysis, 113–117
   early technology used by, 8
   future of, 25–26
   Grassroots '84 series, 48–56
   importance of, 166–167
   index system, 8–10

204 INDEX

C-SPAN *(continued)*
    as media coverage for the people, 48–53
    media maneuverings from insider's view of, 20–25
    metadata, 113–117
    nature and impact of, 16–19
    partisanship and, 155–158
    politics of localism and, 54–56
    programming scope, 7–8
    relationship with Purdue University, 4, 7
    volume of records, 4–5
C-SPAN Archives, xiii
    access to unedited digital content through, xvi–xvii
    clipping and sharing of video, 10–12, 134
    closed captioning, 9–10
    Congressional Chronicle, 94
    contribution to mass communication theory, 125–126
    debate network approach, 110–112, 119–120
    digitization of, 8–9
    EPICS team, 148–150
    George Foster Peabody Award, 8
    indexing, 8–10, 12, 133
    mobile access to, 6
    possibilities for future use of, 150–152
    practice capital approach, 112–113, 117–119
    reasons for edited collection focused on, xv
    record format, 9
    research design, 83–84
    teaching value of, 139
    technology changes affecting, 5–6
    timeliness of, xvi
    transparency and verification using, 96
    upcoming conferences and edited collections, xviii–xix
    used to enhance perceived accuracy of news, 85–86, 89–90
    used to improve media outreach, 84–85, 89–90
    used to measure emotions in public figures, 93–95
    used to provide historical context for current events, 86–88, 90–91
    used to review and improve quality of news, 88–89
    used to teach mass communication theory, 123–132
    utilization for engaged scholarship, xvii–xviii, 3, 5, 93
    vision for, xiv
    visualization tools, 117–119
    volume of records, 4–5
C-SPAN at 34, 94
C-SPAN employees, 83, 89–91
    findings of research using, 84–89
    research design, 83–84
    use of archives to enhance perceived accuracy of news, 85–86, 90
    use of archives to improve media outreach, 84–85, 89–90

C-SPAN employees *(continued)*
  use of archives to provide historical content for current events, 86–88, 90–91
  use of archives to review and improve quality of news, 88–89
C-SPAN Video Library. *See* C-SPAN Archives
Cummings, Elijah E., 66, *66*, 67
Cuomo, Mario, 21
Curiel, Carolyn, 141–142, 144, 175, 176
Curling, Raven, 34

D

Daily Show, 24
Daniels, Mitch, xviii
Dayton, Mark, 96
Debate, 173
  gravitational pull, 114–115
  metadata analysis, 113–117
  network approach to C-SPAN Video Library, 110–112, 119–120
  practice capital approach, 112–113, 117–119
  visualization tools, 117–119
Deepwater Horizon oil spill, 142
Deference, democratic
  American style, 61–65
  costs and benefits of, 72
  language of, 65, 72–75
  mutual versus asymmetric, 72–75
Degeneres, Ellen, 165
Delp, Ed, 149

Democracy for America, 101
Democracy Network, 160
Dochuk, D., 58n4
Dole, Bob, 22
Donnerstein, Edward, 129–130, *130*
Duncan, H. D., 72
Dworkin, Andrea, 167n4
Dyson, Michael Eric, 30, *31*, 33–35, *34*, *40*
  on African Americans as Israel, 40–42
  on Obama as Moses, 35–37
  on Obama as Pharaoh, 37–40, 42–43

E

Economic stimulus, 31–32
Edwards, Mickey, 135
Eisenhower, Dwight, 156
Ekman, P., 102, 104
Elmendorf, Douglas, 116–117
Emotional valence, 104–105
Emotions, 96–98
  anger, 100
  as explanation for people's deviation from normal behavior, 100
  facial recognition technology (FRT) and, 95, 97, 101–107
  importance of research on, 98–100
  psychology of, 100
  research and facial expression, 101
Emotions Revealed: Recognizing Faces and Feelings to Improve Communication and Emotional Life, 102

Engaged scholarship, xvii–xviii, 3, 5, 93
Engineering Programs in the Community (EPICS), 13, 145–147, 176
  C-SPAN Archives team, 148–150
  human-centered design (HCD) and, 147–148
  partnerships and the C-SPAN Archives, 147–150
  possibilities for future C-SPAN archival use and, 150–152
Enron, 5
ESPN, 17
Exodus. *See* Moses, Obama as; Pharaoh, Obama as

F

Facebook, 117
FaceIt, 103
FaceReader algorithm, 104, 105–106
Facial recognition technology (FRT), 95, 97, 101
  early research on, 102–104
  future of, 106–107
  hypothesis, 102
  recent developments, 103–104
  today, 105
  understanding emotional valence and, 104
Falwell, Jerry, 53
Farrakhan, Louis, 33
Fauntroy, Michael, 33
Feingold, Russ, 60, 66, 67
Fenno, R. F., Jr., 74
Financial crisis of 2008, 5
Firing Line, 156

Foley, Tom, 87
Fox News, 16, 18, 21, 164, 166, 167n3
Fox Piven, Frances, 167n3
Franken, Al, 96
Freedom Channel, 160
Freeman, L. C., 112
FRT. *See* Facial recognition technology (FRT)

G

Gastil, John, 63
Geismer, L., 58n4
George Mason University, 143
Giffords, Gabrielle, 161
Gingrich, Newt, 22, 54, 68, *68,* 68–69, 101, 164
Gitlin, Todd, 51–52
Goffman, E., 62, 65, 69
Government, American. *See* American government
Grassley, Charles, 70–71
Grassroots '84
  coverage of Ronald Reagan's campaign, 48–53
  politics of localism and, 54–55
Gravitational pull algorithm, 114–115
Greenberg, B. S., 99
Greenberg, D., 47
Greenwood, Lee, 45
Gunter, Kenneth, 16, 48

H

Habitat for Humanity, 146
Haig, Al, 64
Hannity, Sean, 163

Hart, Gary, 51
Hart, Roderick, 13–14, 77n1, 177
   on family and politics, 155–158
   on importance of C-SPAN for political civility, 166–167
   on uncivil louts, 161–166
   on web evangelists, 157–161
Hart Associates, 94
HBO, 17
Hill, Theon, 12, 173, 174
Hirsch, Donald, xx
Historical context for current events, 86–88, 90–91
Holtzman, Elizabeth, 143
Hoover, Herbert, 63
Horacek, Slade, xx
Human-centered design (HCD), 147–148
Hurricane Katrina, 5, 165

I

Identix, 103
Incivility, political, 161–166
Indexing of videos, 8–10, 12, 133
Iran-Contra Investigation, 5
Iraq War, 5, 70, 96
Israel, African Americans as, 40–42
Istook, Ernest, 135, *136*

J

Jackson, Jesse, 33
Jamieson, Leah, 148
Jaroslovsky, Rich, 50–51
Joint Select Committee on Deficit Reduction Hearings, 114

K

Kellerman, Barbara, 62
Kennedy, John, 99
Kerrey, Bob, 69–70, 72
King, Martin Luther, Jr., 29, 33, 35, 38, 39, *40*, 42
Klein, Ezra, 142
Klein, Joe, 60
Kolers, A., 74
Kowal, Christopher, 13, 174
KredibleNet, 114

L

Lamb, Brian, xiii, xix, 4, 12, 48, 54, 166, 170, 175, 176
   on access to C-SPAN content, 19–20
   on the beginnings of C-SPAN, 15–16
   on C-SPAN's future, 25–26
   on C-SPAN's nature and impact, 16–19
   on media maneuverings from insider's view, 20–25
   Purdue Institute for Civic Communication (PICC), 141–142
Lamprey, S., 57n3
Language of deference, 65, 72–75
Leadership. *See also* Politics
   accommodation and, 69–72
   appreciation and, 65–69
   deference and, 61–65, 72–75
   members of Congress lobbying for committee assignments and, 136–138

Leadership *(continued)*
 mutual versus asymmetric deference and, 72–75
 responsibilities of, 75–77
Lee, Barbara, 70, *71*
Lee, Mike, 73
Lees-Marshment, Jennifer, 63
Leibowitz, K., 99
Lewinsky, Monica, 100
Lewis, John, 167n3
Lieberman, Joe, 66, 71, 96
Limbaugh, Rush, 166
Lind, Colene, 13, 77n1, 173, 174
Listening sessions, 60, 77n2
Lobbying by members of Congress for committee assignments, 136–138
Localism, politics of, 54–56, 57n2, 173
Los Angeles Herald Examiner, 51
Los Angeles Times, 51
Lott, Trent, 60
Lungren, Dan, 67, 71

M

MacDowell, K. A., 98, 99, 100
Malveaux, Julianne, 33
Marcus, G. E., 99
Markle Foundation, 160
Martin, R. S., 46
Marx, Groucho, 62
Mass Communication Research: A Basic Overview, 124–125
Mass communication theory, 123–124
 contribution of C-SPAN Archives to, 125–126

course assignment based on C-SPAN Archives, 130–131, *132*
 course in, 124–125
 Edward Donnerstein on media violence and, 129–130
 future directions, 131
 Joanne Cantor on television ratings and, 128–129
 Tom Wolfe on Marshall McLuhan and, 126–128
Matei, Sorin, 13, 174
McCain, John, 96
McGirr, L., 58n4
McLuhan, Marshall, 125, 126–128
Media outreach, 84–85, 89–90
Media violence, 129–130
Meek, Carrie, *137,* 137–138
Meet the Press, 21
Mehrabian, A., 101
Menken, H. L., 62
Mikulski, Barbara, 72
Milligan, Susan, 64
Moakley, Joseph, *137,* 137–138
Mondale, Walter, 50–51
Morning Grind, 143
Moses, Obama as, 29, 33, 35–37, 40, 42–43. *See also* Israel, African Americans as
Moynihan, Pat, 21
MPAA movie rating system, 128
MSNBC, 16, 18, 96, 166
Murkowski, Lisa, 63, 67, 69
Mutual versus asymmetric deference, 72–75
Myers, D., 98

N

NAFTA, 5
National Communication Association (NCA), xiv, xx, 3, 6, 175
Nationalism, 45–46, 55–56
National Press Club, 49
National Public Radio, 51
National Society of Black Engineers (NSBE), 146
NBC, 142
Need for cognition, 99
Network television, 21
New Right, 46
News
    historical context of current, 86–88, 90–91
    media outreach and, 84–85
    perceived accuracy of, 85–86, 90
    quality of, 88–89
New Strategies Group, 101
New York Times, 16, 33, 82, 119
Nixon, Richard, 100
Noldus FaceReader, 104, 105–106

O

Oakes, Bill, 176
Obama, Barack, 29, 96, 144, 165, 173
    African Americans as Israel and, 40–42
    black discontent in the age of, 31–33
    as Moses, 29, 33, 35–37, 40, 42–43
    as Pharaoh, 37–40
    "racial pass," 32

Oklahoma City bombing, 5
Olbermann, Keith, 164

P

Parry-Giles, Trevor, xx, 175
Partisanship, 155–158
Party identification, 134–135, 156
Pence, Mike, 72–73, *73*
Perceived accuracy of news, 85–86, 90
Persian Gulf War, 5, 82
Pew Research Center, 90
Pharaoh, Obama as, 37–40. *See also* Israel, African Americans as
Phillips-Fein, K., 57n1
Pitkin, Hanna, 63
Playbook, 143
Polar Rose, 103
Politco, 143
Politics. *See also* Leadership
    deference, 61–65, 72–75
    and emotional tone of politicians, 93–95
    facial recognition technology (FRT) and, 95, 97
    of localism, 54–56, 57n2, 173
    media coverage of, 47–48
    members of Congress lobbying for committee assignments and, 136–138
    nationalism and, 45–46, 55–56
    partisanship and, 155–158
    party identification and, 134–135, 156
    and politicians views of C-SPAN, 20–25

Politics *(continued)*
   uncivil louts and, 161–166
   Web evangelists and, 157–161
Ponnaru, Ramesh, 142
Poverty, 32–33
PowerPoint, 134
Practice capital approach to C-SPAN Video Library, 112–113, 117–119
Presidential election, 1984, 45–46
   Grassroots '84 coverage of, 48–56
Presidential election, 2000, 5
Project IMPACT, 141–142
Promised Land. *See* Moses, Obama as; Pharaoh, Obama as
Public Speaking International, 101
Purdue Institute for Civic Communication (PICC), 13, 141–142
   relationship with C-SPAN, 4, 7
   upcoming conferences, xviii–xix
Purdue University, xiii–xiv
   Brian Lamb School of Communication, xx, 3, 6, 124–125, 131
   Engineering Programs in the Community (EPICS), 13, 145–152, 176

R

Rachel Maddow Show, The, 96
"Racial pass," 32
Randall, Michelle, xx
Rather, Dan, 156
Ratings, television, 128–129
Reagan, Ronald, 45, 62, 165
   Al Haig and, 64
   C-SPAN coverage of, 47–48
   Grassroots '84 and, 48–53
   "Morning in America" campaign, 46, 53
   National Press Club speech, 1980, 49
   nationalism resurgence under, 45–46, 55–56
Record format, C-SPAN, 9
Rehnquist, William, 24
Republican Party, 135
Rhetoric. *See* Debate
Roberts, Cokie, 21
Robertson, Pat, 17
Roosevelt, Franklin D., 46
Rosencrans, Bob, 16, 25, 48
Russert, Tim, 21
Rutan, Carl, 54, 55
Ryan, Paul, 64

S

Same-sex marriage, 5, 86–87
Sanchez, Rick, 167n3
Sandy Hook school shooting, 5
Scalia, Antonin, 24
Schieffer, Bob, 21
Scholarship, engaged, xvii–xviii, 3, 5, 93
Scott, Rick, 87
Scully, Steve, 25, 143–144, 175, 176
Sharing and clipping of video, 10–12, 134
Sharpton, Al, 33
Shields, S. A., 98, 99, 100
Showtime, 17
Silverman, F. R., 99
Simons, H. W., 99

60 Minutes, 18
Smiley, Tavis, 30, 33–34, 42, 43–44. *See also* "We Count! The Black Agenda is the American Agenda"
Snow, Tony, 21
Social media, 85, 86, 90, 159
Sparks, Glenn, xiii, 6, 13, 175
Specter, Arlen, 59
Spin, trait-focused, 99
Stanford Research Institute, 103
State of the Black Union, 43
Stelter, B., 82
Stern, Howard, 166
Stewart, Jon, 24, 166, 167n3
Stimulus, economic, 31–32
Stolberg, Sheryl, 33
Stupak, Bart, 74–75
Sugrue, T., 57n2
Summers, M., 57n3
Supreme Court, 23–25
Swain, Susan, xix, 7, 24, 25, 170
Sypher, Howard, xiii, 6

T

Taft, William Howard, 23
Tannenbaum, P. H., 99
Tea Party caucus, 74
Technological determinism, 47
Technology
 closed captioning, 9–10
 early video, 8
 indexing, 8–10
 used by C-SPAN, 81–82
Television. *See also* News
 broadcast, 21, 48, 81

cable, 17–18, 48–49
 coverage of politics, 47–48
 ratings, Joanne Cantor on, 128–129
 violence on, 129–130
This Week, 21
Thomas, Clarence, 5
Thompson, Tommy, 22–23
Tillman, Dorothy, 33
Tingley, D., 98
Town hall meetings, 59–60, 173
 accommodation and, 69–72
 appreciation expressed by politicians at, 65–69
 citizen initiative and, 69–70
 C-SPAN Archives, 61, 76
 deference and, 61–65
 history of, 60
 language of deference and, 65, 72–75
 mutual versus asymmetric deference in, 72–75
 as potentially uncomfortable, 64–65
Townsend, R. M., 67
Trait-focused spin, 99
Transforming Lives, Building Global Communities (TLBGC), 146
Transparency and verification, 96
Troy, G., 57n1
Tulis, J. K., 63
Turner, Ted, 18
Twitter, 85, 159

U

Uncivil louts, 161–166

Universal Facial Expressions of Emotion, 104
USA Today, 51

V
Valence, emotional, 104
Valenti, Jack, 128
Violence, media, 129–130
Visible Effort, 114
Visualizations, 117–119

W
Wall Street Journal, 50
Walters, Ronald, 33
Washington Journal, 85
Washington Post, 21, 143
Watergate, 100
Web evangelists, 157–161
Web pages, 11
Web White and Blue Project, 160
"We Count! The Black Agenda is the American Agenda," 30, 33–34
African Americans as Israel and, 40–42
Obama as Moses and, 35–37
Obama as Pharaoh and, 37–40
Weiser, Irwin (Bud), xiii
West, Cornel, 33
Westen, Tracy, 160
Whirl, Christina, xx
Wilentz, S., 56–57n1
Wilson, Joe, 167n3
Wilson, Steve, xiii
Wolf, Helen, 102
Wolfe, Tom, 126–128, *127*
WYAH, 17
Wyden, Ron, 67–68

Y
YouTube, 144

Z
Zoltowski, Carla, 146, 176